40 DAYS TO A JOY-FILLED LIFE FOR TEENS

THINK
4:8

40 DAYS TO A JOY-FILLED LIFE FOR TEENS

TOMMY
NEWBERRY

with Lyn Smith

Tyndale House Publishers, Inc. Carol Stream, Illinois

Visit Tyndale online at www.tyndale.com.

Think 4:8: 40 Days to a Joy-Filled Life for Teens

Library of Congress Cataloging-in-Publication Data

Newberry, Tommy.
  Think 4:8 : 40 days to a joy-filled life for teens / Tommy Newberry with Lyn Smith.
    pages cm
  Includes bibliographical references.
  ISBN 978-1-4143-8716-1 (sc)
1. Joy—Religious aspects—Christianity. 2. Thought and thinking—Religious aspects—Christianity. 3. Christian teenagers—Religious life. I. Title.
  BV4647.J68N49 2013
  248.8'3—dc23   2013017995

Printed in the United States of America

19	18	17	16	15	14	13
7	6	5	4	3	2	1

*With gratitude, this book is dedicated to the
next generation of 4:8 thinkers.*

CONTENTS

ACKNOWLEDGMENTS

I am thankful for everyone who has read *The 4:8 Principle* and *40 Days to a Joy-Filled Life* and for their encouragement to make this message available and relevant for teenagers. It's finally here!

The book you are reading has incorporated the hard work of many people, and I am grateful for each and every one of them!

Thanks to my agent, Pamela Harty, and to Katara Patton at Tyndale for pulling this project together and making it a reality. I am thankful for Lyn Smith, who beautifully adapted the 4:8 message for younger readers. Ongoing thanks to Karin Buursma for once again expertly polishing another 4:8 manuscript for maximum impact.

I am grateful for my three sons, who inspire me daily—
my mom and dad, whose unconditional love still shapes me—
my wife, Kristin, who encourages me—
and to my heavenly Father, who created me.

ACKNOWLEDGEMENTS

INTRODUCTION

THIS BOOK WASN'T WRITTEN for your mom or dad, although they might become curious enough to peek inside it when they see what it does for you. It wasn't written for your youth leader, teacher, or coach, either.

This book is just for you!

It was written for you because I believe God has an incredible plan for your life, and I want you to live it. Living God's plan has a lot to do with the way you think. During the next forty days, you will be inspired and challenged to upgrade your thinking and refresh your attitude. By following this forty-day game plan, you will erase some weak, unhelpful thinking and replace it with strong, productive thinking. The Bible describes the best way to think like this:

> Fix your thoughts on what is true and good and right. Think about things that are pure and lovely, and dwell on the fine, good things in others. Think about all you can praise God for and be glad about. (Philippians 4:8, TLB)

Over years of coaching others to reach their life goals, I've come to the conclusion that this single verse from the New

Testament contains the secret to a joy-filled life. When you apply this verse to your daily life—transforming the way you think by focusing on your strengths, your blessings, your goals, the people who love you, and the truths of who God is and who he has made you to be—your joy will be amplified. That's what I call the 4:8 Principle.

If you let it, God's way of thinking and this book can totally change your life. Do you know that you don't have to be afraid or insecure? Do you know that what other people say about you doesn't have to define you? Do you know that your thoughts today will impact your future? Do you know that an exciting road that God designed with your name on it now stretches before you?

It's all true. And you can live it. In forty days, you can be on your way to a joy-filled, purpose-driven life.

You can go through this book on your own, but my coauthor, Lyn, and I suggest you read it with at least one other person, and preferably with a group, such as your church youth group. Having other people on a similar journey is encouraging and a lot more fun than going it alone.

However you approach this new experience, my prayer is that mighty things will happen in you and through you. I have every confidence in God that as you learn to think and live the way he intended, he will help you become a Spirit-powered influencer and leader.

Hang on, think 4:8 . . . and let the joyride begin!

THINK THIS, NOT THAT

The Joy of Free Will

Fix your thoughts on what is true and good and right. Think about things that are pure and lovely, and dwell on the fine, good things in others. Think about all you can praise God for and be glad about.
PHILIPPIANS 4:8, TLB

YOUR MIND is a busy place. Some researchers say we have around thirty-five thoughts per minute, adding up to approximately fifty thousand each twenty-four hours. Others think the numbers are much higher: 1,500 thoughts per minute or 1.4 million thoughts per day. Either way, that is a lot of thinking!

Every time you talk or text with friends, you are sharing your thoughts and listening to theirs. When you watch television or read a book, your mind is taking in information. Walking through the halls at school, you think about what you are seeing and hearing. When an adult gives instructions, you decide how you feel about his or her directions and whether you are going to comply with them.

Many of these thoughts flow through your mind quickly. You may not even know you've had them. Yet they are very important. Every single thought affects who you are and what you do.

At any given moment you can choose to

think excellent thoughts, not mediocre thoughts;
think fresh, exciting thoughts, not stale, boring
    thoughts;
think compassionate thoughts, not harsh thoughts;
think loving thoughts, not indifferent thoughts;
think helpful thoughts, not hurtful thoughts;
think grateful thoughts, not entitled thoughts;
think success thoughts, not failure thoughts;
think giving thoughts, not getting thoughts;
think serving thoughts, not self-centered thoughts;
think responsible thoughts, not irresponsible thoughts;
think positive thoughts, not negative thoughts.

These choices impact every area of your life, from how you study, to the amount of confidence you have to try new things, to what you eat, to the quality of your friendships, to how you play sports, to what you wear, to your relationships with your parents. Your thoughts directly affect everything you do.

Your thoughts also reveal who you are. Everything you say,

text, or share on social media reveals your thoughts. The real you shows up even if you don't intend it to. Your thoughts show!

Whatever you give your attention to expands in your life. If you think about your strengths, your blessings, your goals, and the people who love you, then you will attract even more blessings, more love, and more accomplishments. It's a powerful truth!

If you want to be happy and successful—and by that I mean becoming more and more like the person God created you to be—make good choices in your thought life. Think positive things, encouraging things, and kind things. Little by little, your mind determines the person you will become.

LIVE 4:8 :

Work It

Wrong or negative thoughts do not simply go away. They need to be replaced. Think about the person you intend to become. Then, in the right-hand column ("Not That") on the following page, identify a few specific thoughts that are incompatible with that vision. In the left-hand column ("Think This"), identify a handful of thoughts that are compatible and helpful. At the bottom, write a short sentence saying what you will commit to do to improve your thinking.

THINK THIS   **NOT THAT**

Talk It

(Note: You can do this section with a friend, a family member, or your youth group.)

Tell one or two people you trust one good thing you are choosing to think about. Ask if they would like to join you so you can help each other. Send a text in the next twenty-four hours reminding them to think about the good things they shared with you.

Stick It: Thought of the Day

I am free to choose my thoughts.

 Pray It

Jesus, please help me to be aware of my thoughts. Don't let my mind be lazy, but help me to think only about things that are important to you and will lead to your best for me. Amen.

THE CHOICE IS YOURS

The Joy of Decisiveness

[Jesus said,] "Simply let your 'Yes' be 'Yes,' and your 'No,' 'No.'"
MATTHEW 5:37, NIV

DO YOU BELIEVE that God has great plans for your future? If you already follow Christ, you might automatically say yes to that question because you know it is the "right" answer. Right spiritual answers that you don't really believe, however, make no difference in your life. Think carefully about these questions:

If God himself were standing in front of you and promised great plans for you, how would you live from that point forward? Would anything change?

Do you believe that God has great plans for your future?

Pause for a moment, and make sure you have been honest

with yourself. Then consider Jeremiah 29:11: I know the plans I have for you, says the Lord. They are plans for good and not for evil, to give you a future and a hope (TLB). If you accept that God has a great future planned for you, your behavior will reflect that. We live what we actually believe, not what we say we believe.

If God has an incredible future planned for us, we need to prepare for it! Who, when promised a wonderful future, would sulk, complain, neglect their schoolwork, and spend hours of time on mindless entertainment? Often we act as though tomorrow doesn't matter or isn't going to be any better than today. God says tomorrow does matter because he has awesome plans for you! Understanding and accepting that truth will change what you do today.

One of the most obvious character qualities that will develop from believing in a God-blessed future is gratitude. Gratitude is a conscious, deliberate choice to focus on life's blessings rather than its shortcomings. When you focus on your blessings, you feel abundant, but when you focus on what is missing, you feel incomplete. Knowing that God is for you, is working on your behalf, and is guiding you toward a good future enables you to be grateful for what you are experiencing along the way. It is a choice.

The power of gratitude is huge. In fact, it is the main component of a joy-filled life. When you choose to be thankful and you express that thankfulness to God and others, you will find more joy at school, church, sports practice, drama rehearsal, work, and home. You will be happier in your relationships and will be a blessing to others.

Gratitude is also the best way to counteract negative emotions. You cannot be grateful and angry or frustrated at the same time. You have to make a choice. Which one is it going to be? The more things you appreciate today, the more blessings you will notice tomorrow. On the flip side, the less appreciative you are today, the fewer blessings you will tend to acknowledge tomorrow.

Today's focus is making an intentional decision to develop a thankful state of mind. Daily gratitude prepares the way for the great future awaiting you. Your challenge is to take a stand and make a decision right now.

What are you going to do?

Own your joy! Either make the decision to be a grateful person from this point on or make the decision not to be. Now is the time to make a choice. Decide to decide. Are you ready to take a leap of joy? The choice is yours.

LIVE 4:8 :::::::::::::::::::::::::::::::::::

Work It

Write a brief note to God, thanking him for the amazing future he has planned for you.

_____

_____

_____

_____

_____

Talk It

Pull aside a friend, explain your choice to become a grateful person, and say three things for which you are grateful. Ask your friend to tell you three things for which he or she is grateful.

Stick It: Thought of the Day

I am choosing to take a leap of joy.

Pray It

Lord, please help me to begin a daily habit of gratitude. Thank you in advance for the amazing future you have planned for me. Amen.

HUNDREDS OF PROBLEMS, MILLIONS OF BLESSINGS

The Joy of Perspective

I will sing the LORD's praise, for he has been good to me.
PSALM 13:6, NIV

YOUR BEST FRIENDS are your best friends because you really like them. When you think about them, you probably think about their good characteristics first. But if you're honest, you will admit that there are some things about them you don't like very much. Your brother or sister might even have more qualities you don't like than qualities you do!

The more time you spend with a best friend or a sibling, the more you see both the good and the bad. Every relationship will have both. What really matters is what you choose to focus on. If you concentrate on what you do not like about someone else, that relationship will feel negative. In fact, the quality of all your relationships depends on whether or not you focus on what is beautiful, excellent, and worthy of praise in the other person.

All of life is a mixture of good and bad. It is not a fairy tale with a rosy glow and a "happily ever after." Your neighborhood, your school, your church, and your family all have ups and downs, pros and cons. That is real life.

At the beginning of Day 1, you read Philippians 4:8, where Paul challenges us to think about the positives in our lives. Take a look at it from *The Message*:

> Summing it all up, friends, I'd say you'll do best by filling your minds and meditating on things true, noble, reputable, authentic, compelling, gracious—the best, not the worst; the beautiful, not the ugly; things to praise, not things to curse.

Think about this verse carefully for a moment. The very fact that Paul is telling us what we should focus on reveals an important point: we always have a choice. If we didn't, this verse wouldn't be necessary. And if we were naturally positive all the time, Paul would not emphasize this point so dramatically.

Paul is reminding us that we can control our thoughts. He teaches us that with God's help, we can choose good thoughts over bad ones and excellent thoughts over mediocre ones. And that's a good thing, because life is never completely good or completely bad. There will always be some junk, and there will always be some greatness.

You may live in a nice house and have awesome parents but struggle with your schoolwork. Maybe you are an excellent student, but you have a hard time making friends. Or perhaps you are a talented musician or athlete, but you don't like the way you look. You may be the most popular person at school but the most unpopular person in your church youth group.

There will always be things to complain about—but there will always be blessings also. Life is filled with mountaintops and valleys. Even in the valleys, something will always be working really well in your life, and even on the mountaintops, not everything will be perfect. Life is always a mixture of good and bad.

You have hundreds of problems and millions of blessings! Whether you choose to count your blessings or complain about what is wrong with your life is up to you.

LIVE 4:8 :::::::::::::::::::::::::::::::::::

Work It

On the following page, make a list of both your problems and your blessings in the space provided. In the left-hand column, write your current problems. Don't hold back! Include everything that comes to mind. In the right-hand column, identify your blessings—everything you're glad to have and glad not to have in your life.

Talk It

Text your blessings to one or two others and ask them to text you theirs.

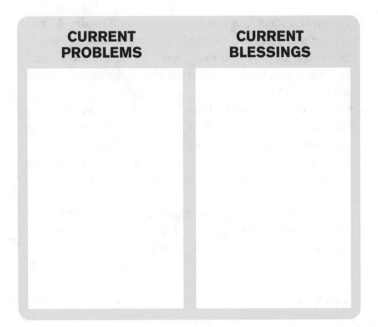

CURRENT PROBLEMS	CURRENT BLESSINGS

Stick It: Thought of the Day

I see the blessings all around me.

Pray It

Read your list to God, telling him how you feel about the problems and thanking him for the blessings.

THE FIFTEEN-MINUTE MIRACLE

The Joy of Daily Solitude

Seek first the kingdom of God.
MATTHEW 6:33, ESV

"GOOD MORNING!" my dad would say enthusiastically as he flipped on the light thirty minutes before I (Lyn) needed to get ready for school. It always seemed too early! That was the pattern in my house, however. We were all expected to be up and reading our Bibles before we did anything else.

While I can't say I always had a good attitude about it, I can say that I am grateful for the habit my parents developed in my life. Now that I make my own choices, I still get up early to read my Bible—because of the joy I get from spending time with God.

The joy-filled life is developed one day at a time. Every morning, you can choose joy. Since God instructs you to seek him first, which produces joy, doesn't it make good sense to have a daily morning appointment with him? When your first priority of the day is your loving heavenly Father, then your day starts on the rock of his truth. Could there be anything more important all day long?

Talk to God and hear from him before you communicate with anyone else. While your mind is peaceful and uncluttered, let God be the first person to influence you.

With tech gadgets at your fingertips, this is a challenge! You may be used to waking up and immediately reaching for your phone. You likely check social media, text messages, and picture sites. By the time you reach for your Bible, your thoughts are far from God, and many other people have put information in your mind.

Since God created you, why not let him help you create your day? He knows you better than anyone else knows you, and he loves you more than anyone else loves you. He has the power to help you achieve your very best! He also knows your family members, your teachers, and your friends. He knows and understands every dynamic in your life. No one else can give you what God can.

Giving God the first part of your morning is one single choice, but it carries with it many good things, including joy, wisdom, and peace. Added to those is the bonus that you will move through the rest of your day with the confidence that you have, for today, sought first the Kingdom of God. That confidence will spill over into your decisions. It will make you bold enough to say yes to the things that you should do and to say no to the things you should avoid. What you do first thing in the morning sets the tone for the rest of the day.

Let's see how you are doing.

How do you normally start the day? Do the first fifteen minutes of your morning focus on God and set you up for a joy-filled day? What do you feed yourself mentally and spiritually after awaking? Just as your body needs a healthy breakfast to give you energy, your mind and heart need time with God. Invite him into your day first thing, and ask him to guide your thoughts and steps.

If you give just fifteen minutes each morning to preparing for joy, it will add up to seven-and-a-half hours in just the first thirty days and about ninety hours in a year. And it can transform your attitude. This is why I call it the Fifteen-Minute Miracle.

LIVE 4:8 :::::::::::::::::::::::::::::::::

Work It

Decide what you will do and what you will need for a morning joy routine. For example, you could use this book, a devotional, and your Bible. Finding a Bible reading plan—either online or in the back of some Bibles—will help structure your reading time. You might want to log your thoughts either in a journal or on your computer. If you like music, pick out some Christian tunes to listen to during your time with God.

Finally, answer these questions: Where will you have your morning joy routine? What time will you get up? What materials will you use? Now you are ready to begin tomorrow morning!

_____

_____

_____

_____

_____

_____

_____

Talk It

Tell a family member or your youth group leader about starting your morning joy routine. Ask him or her to check back with you in a few days to see how it's going.

Stick It: Thought of the Day

I joyfully start each day with God!

Pray It

Heavenly Father, I look forward to starting my days with you. Please help me to get up in time to have fifteen minutes with you. Thank you for how much joy this is going to add to my life! Amen.

THAT'S HOW GOD MADE DOGS

The Joy of Careful Thinking

Be careful how you live. Don't live like fools,
but like those who are wise.
EPHESIANS 5:15, NLT

I (LYN) USED to have two Chihuahuas—brothers named Twitch and Shake (don't you love it?). Twitch was the bigger of the two and quickly positioned himself as the dominant dog. Whatever Twitch did, Shake did. When Twitch jumped off the couch and ran to the back door to go out, Shake was right behind him. If Twitch started barking, Shake joined in. That's how God made dogs. The dominant one acts, and instinctually, the others follow.

God did not create people to be like this. Just because one person acts a certain way does not mean everyone else has to follow automatically. If your brother or sister disobeys your parents, that does not mean that you should too. If another student is disrespectful to a teacher, that does not mean you need to be. If someone says something untrue or unkind about you, that doesn't mean you should do the same to someone else. If your friend cheats on his test, that does not mean it is okay for you to cheat on yours. Wrong responses steal our joy. You don't have to let that happen.

There are two types of thinkers: reactive and proactive. The reactive thinker is like Shake, whose responses were automatic and not thought out. This type of thinking requires no effort at all. You simply show up and react to your circumstances in whatever way comes naturally to you. In some situations, things work out fine. In others, not so much.

By contrast, the proactive thinker gives himself or herself time to plan a response. If you're thinking proactively, you decide that no matter what is going on around you, you are not going to allow it to change what is going on inside you. Nothing and no one but you will determine your responses. You tell yourself things like these truths:

- No matter how I am treated, I will treat others with kindness and respect.
- I want my joy to show no matter how difficult the situation is.
- God can help me to be calm even when there is chaos around me.
- There is no temptation I cannot resist with God's help.

When you overreact to what other people do, or follow along without thinking, you are giving others control over your life. But your life belongs to God! He intends for you to live in a way that honors him. Only in those right choices will you experience his fullness of joy.

You have probably heard someone say, "You make me so mad!" Maybe you've even said it yourself. But that phrase is not true. No one can make you mad without your permission. Other people's actions don't make you respond a certain way. Your response is your choice. If you are angry, you have chosen anger.

To let other people control how you feel and how you respond is a sure way to lose your joy. You don't have to let that happen.

LIVE 4:8 :::::::::::::::::::::::::::::::

Work It

Becoming a proactive thinker means planning ahead. In the spaces labeled "Scenario" on the following page, write three negative or stressful situations you face on a regular basis. Below each situation, first write a negative way you could respond. Then write a positive response based on your verse from Day 1: "Fix your thoughts on what is true and good and right. Think about things that are pure and lovely, and dwell on the fine, good things in others. Think about all you can praise God for and be glad about" (Philippians 4:8, TLB).

SCENARIO 1	SCENARIO 2	SCENARIO 3
poor	*poor*	*poor*
optimal	*optimal*	*optimal*

Talk It

Ask a friend to practice with you. Have him or her describe a stressful situation, and then respond in a positive way. Make it fun!

Stick It: Thought of the Day

I am a proactive thinker, and it shows!

Pray It

God, thank you for how you made dogs and how you made me. Please help me to be a proactive thinker, responding to difficult people and situations in ways that please you. Let my joy show! Amen.

WRITE YOUR OWN STORY

The Joy of Goals

I know the plans I have for you, says the Lord. They are plans for good and not for evil, to give you a future and a hope.
JEREMIAH 29:11, TLB

CELEBRITY GOSSIP, athletes doping, musicians performing in front of screaming crowds . . . We think these stories are so exciting—but really, who cares, when you can write your own life story and make it great?

A great story is written one chapter at a time. And writing chapters that result in a great story involves setting goals for each chapter. The same is true for your life. If there are things you want to accomplish, set specific goals and live those chapters. Goals work because we all enjoy moving toward something we want to experience. That's why it is so much more fun to head off on a vacation than it is to endure the long trip home. Goals give us targets and things to look forward to.

What are your hopes and dreams? Set goals to make them happen. Many people just do whatever is easiest or whatever comes along next. Time passes, and before they know it, their hopes and dreams have died. You don't have to let that happen! Now is the time to start planning the chapters you will write for your life.

You may feel as if you don't have a lot of choices right now, that your life is pretty much planned for you. In a sense that is true, since you are in school and living under the guidance of parents or guardians. But that won't always be the case. Eventually you'll move into a different stage of life and will make your own decisions. Those years will lay the foundation for the rest of your life. Decide now what you want to accomplish in your teens, twenties, and beyond.

Let's get specific. If you want to be the lead in the next drama production or the quarterback on the football team or a cheerleader or the winner of the next science fair, you need to set practice or preparation goals to achieve those objectives. What scores do you want to get on the PSAT, ACT, or SAT exams? What colleges do you want to apply to? Do you need financial aid for college? Are you planning to learn a trade? Set goals for how you will achieve what you want to accomplish. Do research online or at the library to find out about requirements, applications, and deadlines. Talk to your school guidance counselor about how to get into your college of choice or how to pursue a particular career path. Ask him or her to help you set specific goals.

Goals tell your brain what to notice. Imagine a football stadium packed full of fans wearing light gray sweatshirts, all except for ten guys who have painted their torsos bright red. Bold goals stand out in your mind like those guys stand out on the TV screen.

Goal setting disciplines your mind to focus on what is lovely, excellent, and worthy of praise. In addition, your goals reveal what you want to see come true in your life. Having clearly written goals helps you focus your attention on the good things you want, making it easier to control your thoughts. An unwritten goal has no power, energy, or authority in your life. Write it down and make it happen!

Without specific, written goals you will waste mental energy thinking about your fears, doubts, and insecurities. Those thoughts develop negative thinking patterns that steal your joy and lessen the quality of your life. Joy-producing goals are measurable, time bound, and consistent with God's Word. They will help you grow into the person God wants you to become. Becoming goal directed builds your character and disciplines you to say yes to the right things and no to the wrong things.

Do you know that God has goals for you? Not just universal goals for all of us, like knowing him in a deeper way and serving him, but specific goals formulated just for us as individuals. Don't miss them! As you talk to God, work through this book, and read your Bible, listen for how he directs your thinking so that your goals will line up with his. God is writing a great story with your life. Plan and live each chapter well.

God + goals + you = an unbeatable combination!

LIVE 4:8 ::

Work It

Step 1: In the circles below, write your big-dream goals, the ones that could take you a long time to achieve.

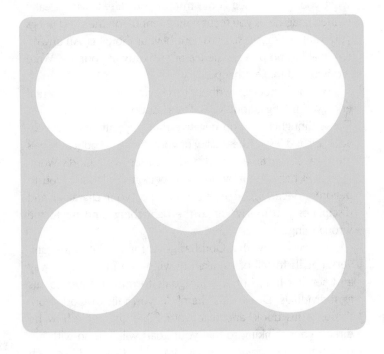

Step 2: On the lines provided, write several short-term goals. For each one, include something you can do this week to get you closer to achieving them.

_____

_____

_____

_____

_____

Talk It

Pick someone you trust—maybe a parent, an uncle, a teacher, a coach, or a youth leader—who has his or her own interesting goals. Then ask for help to define your own goals and plan the action steps to reach them.

Stick It: Thought of the Day

I am goal directed and loving it!

Pray It

Father God, I believe you are writing an amazing story with my life.
Please help me to set goals that will honor you, and help me to stay
focused on them throughout the day. Amen.

FOCUS CREATES FEELING

The Joy of Awareness

As he thinks in his heart, so is he.
PROVERBS 23:7, AMP

WE BECOME what we think about.

In Oklahoma there's a saying, "What's down in the well comes up in the bucket." In other words, what is going on in your mind is what will be lived out in your life. You can determine for yourself what that is.

Every moment, you control your thoughts. You can choose to think about what you have or what you don't, what you won or what you didn't, the person who likes you or the person who doesn't, what brings you joy or what brings you pain, and what's possible or what's impossible.

Whatever you think about becomes more and more important to you. Here's how it works: the more you think about your physical features that you like, the better you will feel about your appearance. The more you work on things you are naturally gifted at, the more confident you will feel in your abilities. The more you think about the good things in your life, the more thankful you will become. The more you look for opportunities to serve others, the more kindness you will receive.

The opposite is also true: the more you think about an unpleasant experience or something that felt unfair, the more frustrated and unhappy you will become. The more you replay in your mind situations that did not go well, the more you will feel discouraged by your life and the people around you.

Do you know people who seem to complain most of the time on social media? Something is always upsetting them. They grumble that something didn't go right, they're mad at their siblings or their parents, they don't want to go to school, they didn't get what they wanted at the mall, someone hurt their feelings, or any number of other negative comments.

Refuse to be like that! Do not keep negative feelings active in your mind, and don't let them spill out onto other people. Stop talking so much about what you messed up or what disappointed you. There is no way around the truth that what you think will determine how you feel and how you live. Do you want to live a great life story like we talked about in Day 6? Then choose to think and talk about the good things in your life. This doesn't mean bragging, but instead saying things that are positive and encouraging. It is thinking about God's presence and blessings in your life. It is talking about your dreams and plans rather than what you don't have or didn't achieve.

Our lives will imitate what we think about the most. In other words, we *feel* what we think about. Our focus determines our feelings.

You train your mind to value what you read, watch, study, and talk about. What absorbs your interest shapes how you think, and whatever holds your attention ultimately determines your behavior. The more you think about something, the more it influences your decisions and actions. The movies and videos you watch, the music you listen to, the books and magazines you read, and the games you play all contribute to your emotional and mental state as well as to the choices you make.

Fix your mind on good things and blessings, in your own life and in the lives of others. If you are tempted to "go negative," remember that it cannot produce anything positive.

LIVE 4:8 :::

Work It

On the following page, write down four positive thoughts you intend to focus on.

Talk It

Share one or two positive thoughts with someone, and ask him or her to text you reminders throughout the week.

1

2

3

4

Stick It: Thought of the Day

My focus creates my feelings.

 Pray It

Jesus, thank you for giving me the freedom to choose my thoughts and feelings. Please help me to think positive things today that keep me on the path toward the awesome future you have for me. Amen.

THE REAL DEAL

The Joy of Knowing Whose You Are

We are God's masterpiece. He has created us anew in Christ Jesus, so we can do the good things he planned for us long ago.
EPHESIANS 2:10, NLT

YOU ARE A BEAUTIFUL, remarkable child of God!

I (Lyn) wish I had believed that. Even when I worked steadily in the modeling industry for several years, I still didn't feel good about myself. I was relying on how I looked in order to be liked and accepted. The problem was that everyone had a different opinion. For every "You're perfect," there were many more "You're too short," "Your hair isn't the right color," or "You don't have the look we want" comments. It was easy to feel like a failure.

When we see ourselves as God sees us and when we let him define us, it is much easier to be happy and confident.

Sadly, many people do not know their true identity in Jesus and consequently miss out on the joy God intended for them.

The way you feel about yourself has been formed over your lifetime. Pictures you have seen, things people have said about you, the way you have been treated, and the standards our culture uses to determine worth all combine to form your self-image. It takes a deliberate and persistent effort to think healthy, productive, and positive thoughts about yourself.

Your true self-worth is based only on what God says about you, not on what others say or how you feel. Think of it this way: if you owned the original of a famous painting but believed it to be only a copy, would that wrong belief determine the painting's actual value? Of course not! You might accidentally sell it for less than it's worth, but that would not change the value of the artwork. The true value of the painting is based on whether it is an original or a copy.

You are an original masterpiece, lovingly made by God. You were not mass produced but were uniquely created. There never has been and never will be anyone just like you. You are one of a kind! Your time here on earth is your special, unrepeatable opportunity to fulfill God's vision for your life and to experience the joy he has placed within you.

Do you see yourself as an awesome child of God? Your true self is not your flesh and bones, but a spiritual being living in a temporary body. The tendency to think less of yourself than God does comes from this broken world. It comes from disagreeing with God. It comes from rejection and defeat. It comes from thinking of yourself as unworthy, unloved, unforgiven, and unwanted. This kind of wrong thinking does you no good!

Remember whose you are. When you see yourself as a child of God, you do not accept other people's wrong opinions of you, you do not allow them to limit the impact of your life, and you do not allow them to steal your joy. This is so important, because how you see yourself limits or expands what God can do with you.

You are a beautiful, remarkable child of God! Think it. Believe it. Feel it. Live like it.

LIVE 4:8 ::::::::::::::::::::::::::::::::::::

 ## Work It

Write three bold statements about what it means to you to be a beautiful, remarkable child of God.

1

2

3

Talk It

Write "You are a beautiful, remarkable child of God!" on three sticky notes. Then say it out loud as you give the notes to three people today.

Stick It: Thought of the Day

I am a masterpiece!

Pray It

Jesus, thank you for making me a beautiful, remarkable child of God. Today, remind me that I belong to you and keep me from dwelling on negative thoughts about myself. Amen.

TAKE A VACATION FROM YOURSELF

The Joy of Shaking It Up

See, I am doing a new thing!
ISAIAH 43:19, NIV

DO YOU EAT the same cereal for breakfast every morning or the same snack after school every day? Do you sit at the same table or even in the same chair during lunch? How about at a party or at your youth group—do you always sit with the same people on the same side of the room? Do you always buy the same gum, drink the same brand of soda, and get the same toppings on your pizza?

That word *same* indicates a groove. If you answered yes to some of those questions, it's likely you are stuck in a groove. Of course, some routines are necessary and good for you, such as brushing your teeth, going to school, and reading your Bible. But other routines are just too comfortable and may be keeping you from experiencing a fuller life.

What might it be like to escape from your rut for a few days or, in other words, to take a vacation from yourself? That's a strange question, right? Obviously you can't get out of your body, but you can hit the "refresh" button on your mind and choices. You can create a mental vacation that reenergizes your life, stirs your creativity, and builds your potential for joy.

One way to do this is by varying some of your habits and thought patterns. Stale thoughts tend to fill your thinking so gradually that you hardly notice the negative effects on your attitude. During this special "vacation," try to cut out criticizing others, any kind of gossiping, and complaining. Don't let the things that bother you come out of your mouth. Refuse to grumble about sore muscles from sports practice, the teacher who assigned a lot of homework, or the long drive to Grandma's house. Take a much needed, healthy, happy break from yourself.

Decide that during this time you will think, speak, and act in a way that is consistent with Philippians 4:8. Keep your mind, as well as your mouth, focused on what is beautiful, excellent, true, just, and worthy of praise. Think about God, talk to God, and forgive others more than you normally do. Speak encouraging words to friends, family members, and even acquaintances. Be brave and defend someone who is being criticized. Say positive things about difficult situations. Think about the good things in your life and thank the people who have made them possible. Review your goals. Take a few moments each day to remember God's character, such as his goodness, kindness, patience, power, love, and forgiveness.

Once your thoughts and words are going in a better direction, it is time to shake up some of your routine. This is only for a few days, so as radical as these suggestions might sound, they are worth a try. If you normally play online games, read a book instead. If you usually read mysteries, try a biography. Instead of going to the same websites every day, ask someone you trust for new ideas. When you open the refrigerator, reach for something different. If you exercise, add a new activity to your routine—try jogging, jumping rope, or running the bleachers. If you are a musician, learn a new song. Text a friend you haven't talked to in a while or initiate a new friendship.

You are smart and creative; come up with some ideas of your own. You may find you really like this mini-vacay and even end up adding new things to your life.

LIVE 4:8 :::::::::::::::::::::::::::::::::::

 ## Work It

What would you do differently if you took a "vacation" from yourself? On the following page, list four changes you would like to make during this mini-vacay.

 ## Talk It

It's much more fun to take a vacation with someone than to go by yourself. Ask someone to join you, pick a starting date, and share your experiences with each other along the way. Consider sharing on social media through pictures or written

1

2

3

4

updates. Maybe you will inspire someone else to take a similar vacation!

 Stick It: Thought of the Day

I am rut free and loving it!

 Pray It

God, thank you for new ideas and for blessing me with so many options. Please free me from stale, useless habits and refresh me with bold, new choices. Amen.

THE SECRET STUDIO

The Joy of Creation

Do not conform to the pattern of this world, but be transformed by the renewing of your mind. Then you will be able to test and approve what God's will is—his good, pleasing and perfect will.

ROMANS 12:2, NIV

THE SECRET to living an exceptional life tomorrow is thinking strong, joyful thoughts today. Filling your mind with great ideas and limitless possibilities will set you free and allow you to thrive as God intends.

There is a war going on in your mind between your human nature and your spiritual nature. Minute by minute, hour by hour, you are contemplating thoughts of good or evil, joy or depression, success or failure. You are writing your own life story with each thought.

When I (Lyn) was in fifth grade, a friend and I passed a note back and forth during class. Our conversation was private—until the teacher saw what we were doing and intercepted a pass. We had written some unkind things that were never intended for anyone else to see. We were in big trouble!

Just as I thought that note was private, you think the top-secret conversations going on in your mind are private. The truth is, your thoughts will eventually be seen. You will live out what you continue to think. Your best and worst decisions begin with one thought.

What you persistently think becomes the words you speak, then the things you do, and eventually the circumstances you help bring about. Today, remind yourself that your thoughts are showing. More than that, your thoughts are shaping your life. Every single one guides you, either toward your God-given potential and joy or away from them. Your thoughts are never neutral. They take you in one direction or the other. Every individual thought matters.

What you are used to thinking about is where your mind will automatically go. If you want to pursue your potential and experience more joy, you have to retrain your mind. Right thinking is your choice and responsibility. God will not force you to think his way; he gives you the freedom to control your thoughts. But when you choose to think Philippians 4:8 thoughts, God will honor your faith and give you the power you need to live a life of excellence. Isn't that amazing? By simply selecting your thoughts, you can shape your life into something spectacular!

In today's verse, Romans 12:2, Paul tells us that we are transformed, or changed, by renewing (starting over, refreshing, repairing) our minds. Check it out in *The Message*:

Don't become so well-adjusted to your culture that you fit into it without even thinking. Instead, fix your attention on God. You'll be changed from the inside out. Readily recognize what he wants from you, and quickly respond to it. Unlike the culture around you, always dragging you down to its level of immaturity, God brings the best out of you, develops well-formed maturity in you.

What happens on the inside of you, in your mind, directly affects what happens in your life. When we focus on God, he will change us! Thoughts filled with God and his good things will lead to more joy. More joy will lead to more accomplishments and better relationships. First allow God to retrain your thoughts and feelings, and then experience God's best for your life.

LIVE 4:8 ::::::::::::::::::::::::::::::::::::

Work It

In the space provided on the following page, write up to five positive statements that reflect the person you want to become. Begin each statement with the words *I am*.

Talk It

Ask someone to be your partner for a day. Text each other this message at least three times: "We are changing the way we think. Positive thoughts only!"

1	
2	
3	
4	
5	

Stick It: Thought of the Day

My thoughts are showing!

Pray It

Jesus, thank you for giving me control over my thoughts. Please help me today to think your thoughts—good thoughts that will change my life. Amen.

DAY
11

THANKSGIVING ISN'T
JUST A HOLIDAY

The Joy of Appreciation

*Be thankful in all circumstances, for this is God's will
for you who belong to Christ Jesus.*
1 THESSALONIANS 5:18, NLT

GRATITUDE RELEASES JOY.

Gratitude naturally draws happy people and pleasant circumstances into your life. When you feel grateful, it means that you have been thinking about the abundance in your life. When you feel unhappy, it is often because you've been thinking about what you don't have. You might have been thinking about a car you want while forgetting that the transportation you have now works just fine. You might have been thinking about that person who doesn't like you rather than all the really good friends you have. You might have been thinking about the one thing your parents don't want you to do instead of the fun things you get to do.

Gratitude changes your mood from sad to happy, from restless to peaceful, and from bored to creative. It enables you to live fully in the present moment, being thankful for the things that are working well in your life right now. Gratitude makes your heart open to joy, which is an unstoppable attitude.

Gratitude is the practice of praise and thanksgiving. A good definition for it is "expressing sincere appreciation to God and to others for the ways that they have benefited your life."[1]

The good news about gratitude is that it can be learned. It is not something you are born with but rather something you train yourself to do. Gratitude involves a decision to focus on your blessings rather than on your shortcomings. When you focus on blessings, your life feels full. When you focus on what's missing, your life feels empty.

I heard this illustration of ingratitude years ago: a man began walking down a street and knocked on the door of the first house he passed. When a woman opened the door, he handed her one hundred dollars. He offered no explanation—just handed her the money and left. The next day he did it again. In fact, he did the same thing for a total of thirty days. On the thirty-first day, he walked past her house, approached another, and knocked on the door. When the door was opened and he handed that neighbor one hundred dollars, the woman in the first house came outside and shouted, "Where's my hundred dollars?"

---

1. *The Power for True Success: How to Build Character in Your Life* (Oak Brook, IL: Institute in Basic Life Principles, 2001), 101.

Did he owe her another hundred dollars? Of course not! The money she had received had been a gift. Unfortunately, she did not focus on the three thousand dollars she had been given, but on the hundred dollars she had not received.

Gratitude is simply a matter of focus and choice. It's a powerful attitude that helps you live a strong and joy-filled life. Are you thankful every day, and do you express that with your words? What kinds of things do you write on Facebook or Twitter? Would your friends, family, and teachers say that you are a grateful person?

Take a moment to consider these questions:

- What is positive and special about your family?
- What are three of your favorite childhood memories?
- What is the nicest thing someone has said to you recently?
- What is the most beautiful thing you have seen in the last week?
- What is the number one thing you are grateful for?

Answering questions like these grows your gratitude and your joy. Have you thanked God for the good things in your life? Do the people you love the most know how grateful you are for them? Remember, gratitude is more than just an attitude. Genuine gratitude needs to be expressed!

LIVE 4:8 ::::::::::::::::::::::::::::::::::

Work It

In the column on the left, write your four favorite blessings. In the column on the right, write the name of the person you need to thank for that blessing.

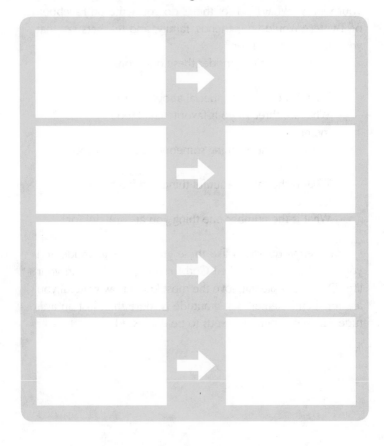

Talk It

Thank the four people you listed in the chart. You can text, write a Facebook note, send a tweet, take a picture of what you are thankful for and post it on social media, write a thank-you note, or call each person on the phone. (If God is the one to thank, offer a prayer to him.) You can probably think of even more ways to express your gratitude!

Stick It: Thought of the Day

I am grateful, and others can tell!

Pray It

Heavenly Father, thank you for how good it feels to express gratitude. Today, please help me to focus on what I have instead of what I don't have. Thank you for my abundance! Amen.

YOUR PARENTS!

The Joy of Honoring

Honor your father and mother. This is the first of God's Ten Commandments that ends with a promise. And this is the promise: that if you honor your father and mother, yours will be a long life, full of blessing.

EPHESIANS 6:2-3, TLB

ONE OF THE BEST WAYS for you to receive God's blessings is to honor your parents. How you treat your parents is so important to God that he made it one of the Ten Commandments! He did not add any qualifications either, such as saying the commandment only applies to nice parents, married parents, rich parents, powerful parents, or Christian parents. All people, everywhere, for all time are commanded to honor their parents. Good things come to those who do.

To honor people means to show them respect, especially when they are a God-given authority in your life. The truth is, your parents were handpicked for you. God chose just the right ones to carry out his bigger plans for your life. Regardless of how it may feel sometimes, you are *not* in the wrong family. God has awesome things in store for you that started with the family he gave you. Your family is not a mistake because God doesn't make mistakes!

The way you think about your parents will help you to honor them. Every thought you have about your mom and dad strengthens or weakens your relationships with them. Respectful, loving, and grateful thoughts will make those relationships better, while angry, resentful, and unhappy ones will make them more difficult.

Thinking unkindly about your parents, even if you believe they deserve it, will not help you at all. If you want more joy in your life, in your home, and in your future, choose good thoughts about your parents. Not only will that help your relationships with them, but it also guarantees God's blessing, because what you think will determine how you behave. If you think kind thoughts about your parents, you also will have kind words and kind actions toward them.

Rotten feelings are not accidental. They flow naturally from the thoughts you continue to stir around in your mind. By mentally replaying unpleasant conversations or situations, you are setting up additional unpleasant conversations and situations. You don't have to do that! You can change your relationships with your parents by the way you think about them and treat them.

Do you think Philippians 4:8 thoughts about your mom and dad? Is every thought about them good, pure, lovely, excellent, and worthy of praise? Does every thought honor God as the one who gave you your parents, and honor your parents in their positions of authority?

Consider how you interact with your mom and dad. Rather than waiting for them to start conversations, you could ask them how their days were or tell them something big or little about yours. When you talk with them, give them your full attention—look at them, take out your earbuds, and put a friendly expression on your face. When your parents give you an instruction or request, honor them by responding quickly and without complaining.

Honoring your parents is a total win for you. Even if they don't seem to appreciate it, God notices—and he's the one who ultimately matters. He will bless your choice to show honor, and you will experience more joy.

LIVE 4:8 :::::::::::::::::::::::::::::::

Work It

On the following page, write three or four positive qualities of your mom, your dad, or both.

Talk It

Either in writing or in conversation, honor your parents by telling them what you appreciate about them.

1

2

3

4

Stick It: Thought of the Day

I honor my
parents, and
they know it.

 Pray It

*Heavenly Father, thank you for my parents. I know they are part of
your good plan for me. Please help me to honor them as you desire.
Amen.*

IT'S CONTAGIOUS

The Joy of Curiosity

Satisfy us in the morning with your unfailing love, that we may sing for joy and be glad all our days.
PSALM 90:14, NIV

IT IS THE GREATEST attitude in the world!

People who have it stand out in a crowd. There is something different about them. They are happy on the outside, with noticeable peace on the inside. Sometimes these people are in hard situations, but they say positive things, encourage other people, and love life.

This attitude is the result of a decision that is nurtured with right thoughts. It will be tested through disappointments and even failure, but it cannot be taken away. What is this attitude? You know it.

It's . . . joy!

Believing that God has great plans for you and your future affects your attitude and fills you with joy. You can't hide real joy; it cannot be contained. Joy is what people see on the outside that is a result of internal faith. It is a way of acting that gives evidence of the spiritual growth that has taken place in your mind and heart.

Joy is a gift from God that comes from trusting him. Romans 15:13 says, "May the God of hope fill you with all joy and peace as you trust in him, so that you may overflow with hope by the power of the Holy Spirit" (NIV). God fills you with joy as you believe him and trust his plans for your life.

Joy is not something you arrive at later; it is a path you choose to walk each day. As you agree with what God says in the Bible and live those truths, you will experience joy. Joy isn't just for adults, successful people, professional athletes, celebrities, the president of your student council, the kid with the hottest car, the captain of the soccer team, the popular kids, or the smartest student at school. Joy is for you. Today!

When you see people having a really good time, you want to know why, right? You become curious. What are they doing that is so much fun? What is their secret? When you go to a restaurant and see a gooey ice cream dessert get delivered to the table nearby, you want to know what it is so you can order one. When your friend gets a high score on his test, you want to know how he studied so you can try it. When a girl wins every race, you ask her how she trains so you can follow the same workout schedule. When you see a table of kids laughing, you want to join in or have fun with your own group.

Joy is contagious. That is especially important for a Christian because it is often your joy that draws people to you and then to

Jesus. Your example speaks louder than any words you say. The expression on your face is either attractive or unattractive. What you do is either attractive or unattractive. The example you set either draws people toward Jesus or pulls them away from him.

God says that living with joy is his will for you (see 1 Thessalonians 5:16-18). It is a big part of God's plan for your life. Being filled with joy doesn't mean your life is perfect, but it does mean that you trust God with your life regardless of what's happening.

This is your one shot at life. These are the only teenage years you get. Choose joy! Live in such a way that people who watch you will be curious. Make them want what you have.

LIVE 4:8 :::::::::::::::::::::::::::::::::::

Work It

In the space provided, describe how you could better express joy so that others see it. Then write "Smile" on a sticky note and put it on your bathroom mirror. Practice makes perfect!

_____

_____

_____

_____

_____

_____

Talk It

Remember this phrase—"A joyful heart makes a cheerful face" (Proverbs 15:13, NASB)—and share it with two people today. Write it down if that helps you.

Stick It: Thought of the Day

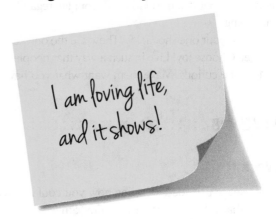

I am loving life, and it shows!

Pray It

Jesus, thank you for wanting me to be joyful and for making your joy available to me. Today, please help me to think, speak, and act so that I draw more people to you. Amen.

MAKING EVERY MOMENT COUNT

The Joy of Right Now

We take captive every thought to make it obedient to Christ.
2 CORINTHIANS 10:5, NIV

ONE OF THE MOST wonderful gifts God has given you is your brain. He designed it to be incredibly powerful. And as part of your free will, he gave you the ability to control your brain. You can use this ability to maximize your God-given potential, or you can abuse it. The way you think can either multiply your gifts and talents or shrink them.

The Bible clearly teaches that we harvest what we plant. "Don't be misled; remember that you can't ignore God and get away with it: a man will always reap just the kind of crop he sows!" (Galatians 6:7, TLB). This is a simple concept, but one we often try to ignore. In farming terms, we plant first, and later we harvest what has grown. The seeds the farmer sprinkles into the soil determine the plants that will grow—and the crop he or she will reap later.

Nowhere is this concept more obvious than in our thinking. As hard as you might try, you cannot think one thing and experience something else. You cannot think negatively and expect to live positively any more than you can plant apple seeds and expect to pick oranges. If you want to live a joy-filled life that fulfills God's good plans for you, then you must keep your thoughts fixed on the things of God.

You cannot be filled with joy if you are worrying. You cannot be confident if you are thinking fearful thoughts. You cannot be hopeful and happy if your mind is full of sad things. You cannot act lovingly toward someone if you feel angry or resentful. Positive and negative thoughts cannot be in your mind at the same time. It is a choice you make every moment.

Your life is happening right now, so how you live this moment counts. You may be in the habit of daydreaming about a different life or wishing things were different. Those are wasted moments because daydreaming and wishing do not change anything. Living each moment fully, while thinking and doing things God's way, produces immediate joy and future success.

If you want to get good grades, you need to sow seeds of good study habits. If you want to make a friend, you need to sow seeds of kindness. If you want to grow a bank account, you need to sow seeds of saving, not spending. If you want the fruit of God's blessing, you need to sow seeds of time spent with him. The choice to sprinkle your best seeds in every moment will be rewarded with a huge crop!

So how are you using your brain? God has given you a powerful mind. Use it wisely to keep your thoughts on the good stuff, and you will make every moment count.

LIVE 4:8 :::::::::::::::::::::::::::::::::::

Work It

What do you think about most of the time? In the left-hand column, write three negative thoughts that bother you the most. In the right-hand column, write three positive things you can think about instead.

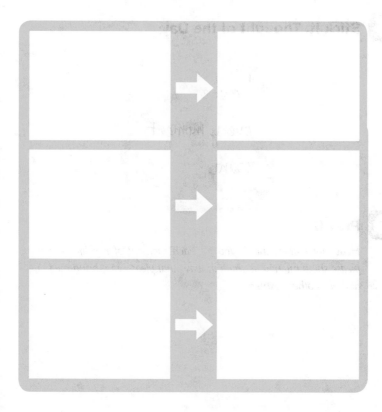

Talk It

Look in a mirror and talk to yourself about the negative things you wrote. Give yourself only five minutes to talk it out. When those five minutes are up, you are done with negative thoughts and words for the day. Now your mind is free to choose productive, healthy, joy-filled thoughts. Make it your goal today to tell someone else the three positive things you wrote down.

Stick It: Thought of the Day

I make
every moment
count.

Pray It

Heavenly Father, thank you for each moment of my life. Today, please show me how to think in ways that please you, bring me joy, and bless others. Amen.

SPEAK UP

The Joy of Words

Watch the way you talk. Let nothing foul or dirty come out of your mouth. Say only what helps, each word a gift.
EPHESIANS 4:29, *THE MESSAGE*

WHOEVER CAME UP with the phrase "Sticks and stones may break my bones, but words will never hurt me" was wrong. Words are powerful! James 3:5-6 compares what words can do to the way a huge forest fire can be started by a tiny spark. It doesn't take much to burn the whole forest to the ground. The same can be true of our speech. Just a few harsh or critical words can hurt someone deeply.

James goes on to talk about how inconsistent it is for us to praise God and curse other people with the same mouth. We need to choose carefully what we say. After all, what comes out of our mouths reveals important things about us.

Your speech reveals your character. In fact, what you say about someone else reveals more about you than about the person you are talking about. If you are a secure, confident person, then your words about others will generally be kind. If you feel insecure about yourself, then you will likely say things to make others look bad. Do your words about others show kindness and thoughtfulness? Do they reveal positive or negative thoughts about others? What do your words say about you?

Crude language and swear words are lazy. Using a varied vocabulary and helpful words shows creativity and intelligence. Let your speech reflect the incredible way God made you. You are not junk! You are the product of brilliance. You were designed and created by the smartest, wisest, most intelligent being that has ever been and will ever be. Think, live, and speak in ways that reflect how amazing you are and how amazing God is!

Polite, considerate words show respect for those listening. When you choose politeness, you are expressing that you value the other person. When you address adults by their appropriate titles, you show respect for their age, experience, and knowledge. If you want others to treat you with respect, speak to them respectfully. Words can produce an echo—what you say comes back at you. Honoring words go a long way toward developing healthy relationships.

God tells us to say things that build up and encourage other people. In fact, today's verse specifically instructs us to say things that will help someone else and to consider our words as gifts. With everything you say to others, you have the opportunity either to contaminate them or contribute to them. You can make their day better or worse. You can give someone the courage to try something new or you can make him feel like a failure. You can speak words of hope to a friend who is discouraged or you can agree that her situation is bad. Your words can have a tremendous impact.

What you talk about and how you talk reveal what is important to you. If you want God's best for your life, and if you want joy, then your speech will be filled with good things. The more honoring and beautiful your words, the more Jesus will shine from your life, and the happier you will be. The more you bless others with your speech, the more God will bless you. The more you let him have control over your thoughts and words, the more power you will experience in your life.

Speaking kindly is never the wrong thing to do. Beautiful words are always the right choice.

LIVE 4:8 :::::::::::::::::::::::::::::::::

Work It

Circle *True* or *False* for each statement:

True *False* I was designed creatively and intelligently so I can use creative, intelligent words.

True *False* My words reveal what I think.

True *False* God will bless me when I bless others with kind words.

True *False* Using honoring words will bring me joy.

True *False* I want to be a person whose words contribute to others.

True *False* I commit to making beautiful words part of my daily speech and to getting rid of words that are crude, unkind, or disrespectful.

Talk It

Text something encouraging to two friends. Also, tell someone you trust that you want to be a person whose words honor God and others.

Stick It: Thought of the Day

My words encourage others!

Pray It

Father God, thank you for the gift of speech. Please help my words to be sources of encouragement and support. Shine through every word I say today. Amen.

FEELING VS. FACT

The Joy of the Truth

Your love is ever before me, and I walk continually in your truth.
PSALM 26:3, NIV

THE HOUSE I (LYN) GREW UP IN was a beautiful, old two
story with a winding, wooden staircase. At the bottom of the
staircase was a post with a flat top that you could put your
hand on as you rounded the corner. We had several cats that
liked to sit on that post. My grandmother, who lived with us
and couldn't see well, would get irritated when she reached
out to put her hand on the post and found a cat in the way.
Eventually she got in the habit of swatting at the post without
even feeling to find out if a cat was there. One day when my
mom came home, she took off her fur hat and placed it on

the post for a few moments while she put other things away. Of course my grandmother came downstairs right then. She reached out, swatted that hat, and sent it sailing across the living room. I will never forget how hard my dad laughed as the hat flew by.

My grandmother had trained herself to react with irritation, regardless of whether or not a cat was in the way. It's easy for us to do this with our feelings, as well. We can train ourselves to react in a certain way, even if that reaction isn't based on reality. We cannot always trust our emotions to fit with the facts.

The biggest mistake we make when we have painful feelings is assuming they are based on the truth. One of the keys to joy is learning to value what is true and right simply because it is true, not just because it feels true. By discovering the truth of what God says about us, we can avoid false feelings and beliefs.

Have you ever taken a dirty air filter out of a car or cleaned off the lint filter in your clothes dryer? Those filters stop dust from getting into the engine of the car or keep lint from getting all over the clothes. Their job is to separate the bad from the good. In the same way, God's Word works like a filter for your feelings, showing you which are based on truth and which are not.

Today we often hear things like "If it feels good, do it," "Whatever makes you happy," or "Let your heart be your guide." Sadly, when we let our feelings lead us, we often go the wrong way. Our feelings are reactions to our circumstances; they have not necessarily gone through the filters of God's Word or our minds. We often assume that because we feel something, it is right, but often there's another explanation altogether. Take these examples:

You are shopping at the mall when you see a friend walking toward you. As you start to wave, she walks right by. Because you have been ignored by a friend before, you immediately feel ignored again. However, the truth is that her mom had just called and told her to hurry home. She was so focused on getting to her car that she was not looking at the people around her. You had an automatic reaction based on a misunderstanding, not on the truth.

You recently recovered from the flu. During the big game, the coach pulls you out and benches you. Because you have been benched before for messing up, you automatically feel like a failure. The truth is, the coach knows you haven't been feeling well and is giving you a break to rest so you'll be able to come back in later and help the team. Your feelings of failure are a faulty reaction to an act of thoughtfulness.

Most of us have feelings that are habits, and those feelings tend to pop up even when they are the wrong response to a situation. These kinds of feelings keep us from the joy-filled life and from happy relationships.

You can shape your feelings by the way you choose to think. If you think good, kind, generous, helpful thoughts, then your feelings will be positive. If you remember that you are a stunning, radiant creation of God, loved and special, you will feel good about yourself and about others. Reading your Bible still is the best way to stay grounded in what is true.

How is your "feelings filter" working?

LIVE 4:8 :::::::::::::::::::::::::::::::::::::

Work It

Draw lines from the negative feeling to the correct positive truth.

I feel lonely.   God knows everything about me.
I feel stupid.   God accepts me.
I feel unloved.   I have everything I need in Jesus.
I feel rejected.   God is never disappointed in me.
I feel untalented.   God is always with me.
I feel inadequate.   I have the mind of Jesus.
I feel like a failure.   God's peace and confidence
I feel like a   fill me.
    disappointment.   God can turn my mistakes into
I feel nervous.   good.
I feel like no one   I have been gifted for a purpose.
    understands.   God loves me every moment.

Talk It

Use the Work It section as a verbal exercise. Have a partner say the negative feeling to you, and then respond with the positive truth. (You don't have to remember the truths word for word; this isn't a memorization exercise. You just need to be able to express the truth in a way that works for you.) Then switch and do the same thing for your partner.

Stick It: Thought of the Day

I filter my
feelings through
God's truth.

 Pray It

Jesus, thank you that I am not my feelings. Today, please help me to value what is true and right simply because you say it is. Let your truth have power over my feelings. Amen.

HUNTING RATS

The Joy of Being Battle Ready

Be strong in the Lord and in his mighty power. Put on the full armor of God, so that you can take your stand against the devil's schemes.
EPHESIANS 6:10-11, NIV

WITHOUT REALIZING IT, we do a lot of silly things that increase our negative feelings. As a result, we end up getting more of what we don't want. We pick the wrong things to think about! Philippians 4:8 clearly tells us what we should do: think on the things that are good, that are working well, and that are worthy of praise. In other words, think about the good stuff. Every life has good stuff, including yours.

When you feel sad or discouraged, you can be pretty sure that you have been thinking on the not-so-good stuff. Some negative thoughts stand out more than others. These "Really Awful Thoughts," or what we will call RATs for short, lessen your potential for joy. Once you realize what they are, you can take them out of your life! Keep in mind that these RATs highlight crooked *thinking patterns*, not crooked people. See if you can relate to any of these patterns:

Amplifiers make unpleasant situations sound worse by using extreme words like always, never, no one, and every time. The truth is, very few things in life are that extreme.

Feelers let negative feelings rule without asking whether or not they are true. Often what we feel is far worse than the reality of the situation. While feelings are important, they should not replace the truth.

Guessers pretend they know what other people are thinking, and they tend to assume the worst. This is not fair to others and can lead to arguments and hurt feelings.

Exaggerators make small difficulties sound huge with words like horrible, worst, terrible, and hopeless. Everything is dramatic. Enter the drama queen or king.

Identifiers take things too personally and assume negative events are attacks against them. For example, your locker door often sticks and is hard to open. When you're in a hurry, you get frustrated and say things like, "They gave me this rotten locker on purpose because they don't like me."

Forecasters loudly predict that the worst will happen even before they get started. They look at the pieces

that need to be put together for the lab project and
immediately say, "No matter how we make this, it
won't work."

Gloomies have the special talent of finding something
wrong, even if it is the only thing wrong. Their mental
radar sees the bad stuff first. Their reward for finding
the bad stuff is that they get to be more miserable.

Blamers point the finger at someone else for their own
problems. It is a popular behavior because it feels
good for a while. Eventually, though, the problems
will have to be dealt with and they will have to take
some responsibility. All blaming does is prolong the
problem and make it worse.

Justifiers remind themselves and others that they deserve
to be miserable and unhappy. They use phrases such
as, "If you only knew what they did," and "I deserve
to be upset."

None of these behaviors produce joy. In fact, they are joy
stealers. As you know by now, you don't have to think, talk,
and act that way. You can protect and even grow your joy and
success by getting rid of the RATs.

Now that you know what the RATs look like, we'll talk
more in Day 18 about how you can erase these negative patterns from your life.

LIVE 4:8 :::

Work It

What Really Awful Thoughts (RATs) bug you? Write down the three you have the most trouble with.

1

2

3

Talk It

This is between you and God. Tell him which RATs you struggle with, and ask him to help you replace those thoughts and behaviors with his.

Fill in the blanks with the three RATs you wrote in Work It.

I do not want to be a(n) _____.
I do not want to be a(n) _____.
I do not want to be a(n) _____.

 ## Stick It: Thought of the Day

I am a
RAT-free
zone.

 ## Pray It

Jesus, thank you for loving me enough to show me where I am losing joy and success. Today, please help me to avoid bad habits I might slip into and choose new, positive responses instead. Amen.

ADMIT AND CHALLENGE

The Joy of Right Feelings

Look deep into my heart, God, and find out everything I am thinking.
PSALM 139:23, CEV

YOUR FEELINGS follow your focus—so if you want to change your feelings, change your focus. Your emotions allow you to feel what you've been thinking about. Feeling positive about life is a good indicator that your recent thinking has been good and healthy.

Feeling great about your life does not mean that it is 100 percent wonderful. Instead, it means you are focusing on the parts of your life that are going well, while at the same time not focusing on what you don't like. But when you experience a few negative words or an unpleasant situation, you can quickly lose the Philippians 4:8 focus. You can easily start feeling as if life is pretty rotten. This is where your choice of focus becomes so important.

Many people living on very little have a lot of joy. When I (Lyn) recently traveled through the African country of Nigeria, I was amazed at the joy and smiling faces. The people who lived in one-room houses with no electricity and no indoor plumbing were some of the happiest, friendliest people I have seen. They live without computers, TVs, techie gadgets, expensive tennis shoes, and cars. Their daily desire is food and water, yet they choose joy. They value people, not things.

On the flip side, many people who have been given a lot are lonely and unhappy. Clearly, how you feel is not based on what you have but on what you choose to value and think about.

To live the life you really want, let your goals and your mind—not your feelings—guide you. To grab hold of all the joy you can, learn how to lessen negative feelings and thought patterns—like the RATs we discussed yesterday—so they do not control your life.

The two most common ways people deal with negative feelings are keeping these feelings buried inside, which makes the people sick and miserable, or letting these feelings explode onto other people, which damages relationships. Many people don't know any alternatives, but *you* don't have to respond like this.

Think about it this way: you are around a campfire making s'mores with your friends. When it is time to go, one of your friends dumps a bucket of dirt on the fire to snuff it out. Since her goal was to stop the fire from burning, she didn't toss another log on it or pour on gasoline. That would have caused the fire to burn hotter and longer. She didn't ignore it either, hoping it would burn itself out. To ensure a fun experience for everyone and to prevent any damage, she made the right, safe, healthy choice to snuff out the fire.

Negative feelings are similar to that campfire. How do you extinguish them? You snuff them out with positive, helpful thinking. If you think more negative thoughts or just ignore your feelings, you only cause them to grow out of control.

If you want positive thoughts that will lead to joy and success, here are two things that will help you: first, admit your negative feelings. Are you afraid or do you feel threatened in some way? Do you feel unloved, disrespected, or rejected? Are you angry? Sometimes negative feelings surface when you have an unmet need such as being tired or hungry. They can also pop up when you are physically uncomfortable, such as having a headache or a cold. If there is a need you can address, take care of it. Take a nap or get a snack. But if your negative feelings were brought on by your thoughts or interactions with someone, move on to the next step.

Second, challenge the feeling. Don't just accept it. Remind yourself, *This is just the way I feel. It's not necessarily the truth. I don't have to act on this feeling.* Feelings are not meant to run your life. God and the truth in his Word are!

Don't be a pushover for negative feelings. Put them in their place—snuff them out with positive thoughts—so that they do not affect your decisions.

LIVE 4:8 :::::::::::::::::::::::::::::::::::::

Work It

Being aware of your negative thought patterns helps lessen their power. In the left column, write down three of your most common negative feelings. To the right, write the things that tend to trigger those feelings.

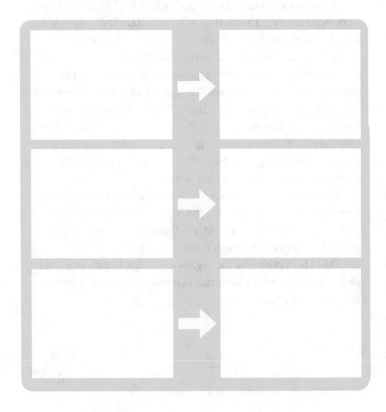

Talk It

Write this on a note card or piece of paper: "This is just the way I feel. It's not necessarily the truth. I don't have to act on this feeling." Say it out loud several times and then carry the note with you all day. Look for an opportunity to share it with someone.

 Stick It: Thought of the Day

My feelings
don't rule my life.
God does!

 Pray It

God, thank you for giving me the courage to admit and challenge my feelings. Please help me to remember that they do not control my life. You do. Amen.

JUST EXCHANGE IT

The Joy of an Easy Return

I have hidden your word in my heart, that I might not sin against you.
PSALM 119:11, NLT

UNWANTED THOUGHTS don't go away just because you tell them to. In fact, resisting unwanted thoughts only puts more focus on them and keeps your mind stuck. As we talked about in the campfire example on Day 18, trying to fight or ignore unwanted thoughts won't work. The only way to do away with negative thoughts is to exchange them for positive thoughts.

Your mind never stops. While you are awake, your brain is active and thinking—and your thoughts are either helpful or hurtful. If you do not intentionally pursue good thoughts, the wrong ones will take over like weeds in a deserted garden.

Because your mind holds only one thought at a time, that thought is either contributing to your life or contaminating it. The good news is that you can control it. You can exchange an average thought with a brilliant thought, or a fearful thought with a courageous one. You don't have to let a harmful thought stay in your mind. It's always an option to exchange it with something better.

If you get angry at your brother or sister and tell yourself not to be mad, you will stay mad. Your mind is focused on the negative feeling of anger, so you will continue to feel upset even if you tell yourself not to. It's like when someone says, "Don't think about breathing." What do you immediately think about? Breathing. Your mind will stay there automatically unless you replace that thought with something else. If you have skied, snowboarded, or skateboarded, you know that when you get up after a nasty fall, you don't keep thinking about what happened. Instead, you focus on your position and balance so you can stay up. You think about what to do *right* rather than what you did *wrong*.

Learning to replace harmful thoughts with helpful ones is what the Bible calls overcoming evil with good. The best way to do that is to meditate on Bible verses. When your mind is full of God's words, it is easier to think good, joyful, successful thoughts. Not only that, but God's words have power! They can help you avoid sin, dangerous situations, and harmful relationships. They can fill you with wisdom, confidence, encouragement, and courage. Look at what God says about Scripture: "The word of God is alive and powerful. It is sharper than the sharpest two-edged sword, cutting between soul and spirit, between joint and marrow. It exposes our innermost thoughts and desires" (Hebrews 4:12, NLT).

When you put God's words in your mind, they always are active. They have the ability to keep working quietly in your heart and mind, even when you don't know that it's happening.

As you read this book and explore the Bible, you will find many helpful verses. Pick one to start with, such as Philippians 4:8, and begin memorizing. You will be amazed at how easy it is. When you store God's truths in your mind, you will begin to discover new joy and new strength you didn't know were possible. Here are a few suggestions:

- Trust in the LORD with all your heart and lean not on your own understanding; in all your ways submit to him, and he will make your paths straight. (Proverbs 3:5-6, NIV)
- You will keep in perfect peace all who trust in you, all whose thoughts are fixed on you! (Isaiah 26:3, NLT)
- You will know the truth, and the truth will set you free. (John 8:32, NLT)
- I have come that they may have life, and have it to the full. (John 10:10, NIV)
- I can do everything through Christ, who gives me strength. (Philippians 4:13, NLT)
- God has not given us a spirit of fear and timidity, but of power, love, and self-discipline. (2 Timothy 1:7, NLT)

You don't need to keep thinking about whatever is holding you back or not producing joy. If you want to have control over your feelings, take control of your mind. Build a better attitude one thought at a time. You hold the power. If your thoughts aren't working for you, it's time to exchange them.

LIVE 4:8 :::::::::::::::::::::::::::::::::::

Work It

Nothing pushes out bad thoughts like God thoughts! Choose two Bible verses you are going to memorize. I suggest you put them into your phone or write them on cards or sticky notes that you can carry with you and see often. Reread them and say them out loud ten to twenty times a day until you have them locked in your mind. Do you want to know one of my secrets to memorizing verses? I write the verse on a card, put it in a waterproof baggie, and keep it in the shower. It's easy to memorize while I shampoo my hair!

_____

_____

_____

_____

_____

_____

_____

_____

_____

_____

Talk It

This is too good to keep to yourself. Say your verses out loud to someone, either while you are still working on them or when you have them fully memorized. Even better, find someone who will memorize them with you.

When a negative thought starts camping out in your mind, begin repeating whatever parts of the verses you have memorized. Exchange those negative words for God's.

Stick It: Thought of the Day

I think God thoughts all day long!

Pray It

Jesus, thank you for giving me feelings so I can experience you and all the good things you have given me. Please help me to enjoy the right feelings and replace the harmful ones with your truth. Give me the power to memorize your words, which will change my mind and my life. Amen.

PICTURE IT

The Joy of Imagination

*God can do anything, you know—far more than you could ever
imagine or guess or request in your wildest dreams!*
EPHESIANS 3:20, *THE MESSAGE*

DID YOU KNOW that you visualize every day? Visualization is a
word that means "imagining the future." Every person imagines
the future many times a day.

Small children visualize being police officers or ballerinas.
High school students visualize graduating and going to college.
Student athletes visualize playing professional sports. College
students visualize exciting careers. Young adults visualize the
person they will marry.

An important part of grabbing hold of what God has for
you is using your imagination carefully. Rather than letting

random pictures float around your mind based on your experiences, movies you've seen, or the mood you are in, take control of your imagination.

God designed you with the ability to picture a better future—to imagine things as they *could* be, not just as they are. This is most obvious when we pray. We are always led to pray for something better, not for something worse. Have you ever heard anyone pray for a bad grade on a test? Or that they would get sicker rather than healthier? Of course not! God gave us the ability to hope for, plan for, and imagine something better. People are the only part of his creation who can do that.

As long as you fix your mind only on what you have and who you are today, you will likely have and be the same thing tomorrow, the day after that, and the years after that. If you only picture the past and the present, you probably won't experience much that is different. As the saying goes, if nothing changes . . . nothing changes.

Sadly, many people spend more time visualizing what they don't want than what they do want. Their minds are stuck, either because they are afraid or because they don't know the awesome plans God has for them. But you know! You know by this point that God designed and created you for a purpose. He has plans for you that you can start picturing now. The power to visualize your future is yours to use or not.

Visualization is used by successful people in all fields, especially in athletics, entertainment, and medicine. It works because of the way God made our brains. The brain tends to fulfill its main thought. What you think about the most and what you most frequently picture happening will tend to take place. Not in some mystical way, but because you will live out whatever you set your mind on.

If you want to live out God's wonderful plans for you, then you need to train your mind to picture the person you know God wants you to become. This starts with Philippians 4:8: "Fix your thoughts on what is true and good and right. Think about things that are pure and lovely, and dwell on the fine, good things in others. Think about all you can praise God for and be glad about" (TLB). Think about having fun with your friends, getting along with your family, using your talents, and becoming even closer to God. Believe it! His vision for you is definitely pure, lovely, good, and right—even way beyond your ability to imagine it!

To get started, every day you need to visualize yourself living a joy-filled life. See yourself doing what you love to do, having a good attitude, and enjoying your friends and family. Picture those things as clearly as you can.

The two best times to practice visualization are right before you go to sleep and just after waking up in the morning. It is kind of like stepping into your own mental movie. In your mind, watch yourself doing what you would be doing if all your prayers were answered and all your goals were met. If you train your mind to hold on to those pictures and you trust God's good plans for you, that visualization is likely to come true. Every day, you'll be growing a little closer to the person he designed you to be.

LIVE 4:8 :::::::::::::::::::::::::::::::::::

Work It

Imagine using your talents to do something that's really important to you and that you know would please God. Picture what that would look like. Write a short paragraph describing who is in your picture, what you are doing, and what the results are.

_____

_____

_____

_____

_____

_____

_____

_____

_____

_____

_____

_____

Talk It

Before you go to bed tonight, read the paragraph you wrote and visualize it again. Tell God that you want his plans for your life, and that for now, this is what you think they might be. Ask his blessing on your talents and desires. Do the same thing again in the morning.

Stick It: Thought of the Day

I picture the awesome future God has for me.

Pray It

Father God, thank you for giving me the power to picture life as it could be rather than just as it is right now. Please help me to visualize things that will move me closer to the person you created me to be. Amen.

A CRY FOR HELP

The Joy of Compassion

Be kind and compassionate to one another, forgiving each other,
just as in Christ God forgave you.
EPHESIANS 4:32, NIV

YOU ARE HALFWAY through your forty days. Congratulations! How are you doing so far? Are you experiencing more joy in your life? Are you replacing negative thoughts with positive ones? Be encouraged! Any progress you make is moving you forward and getting you closer to your goals.

Up to this point, we have talked mostly about ways you can change your own thoughts and attitudes. But that only goes so far, since there are other people on the planet. They can be fun or frustrating. They can add good things to your life, or they can try to drain away your joy. How do you respond? One simple word: *compassion.*

Compassion means understanding that other people have needs and that they are not perfect. Having compassion toward others is like having the heart of God for them. It involves loving them like God loves. Psalm 103:13 explains, "As a father has compassion on his children, so the LORD has compassion on those who fear him" (NIV). The Gospel of Matthew mentions several times that when Jesus saw people, he had compassion on them. He understood that they had needs and knew that he could help them. We are to be like Jesus, so that means we are to have compassion.

You have nothing to lose and everything to gain by choosing compassion. In other words, it's all good. Here's how it works: you don't ignore the negative feelings you have toward others, but you change them into positive feelings of compassion instead. If certain people are irritating you, are in your way, or are rude to you, assume they are unhappy. Give them the benefit of the doubt and assume that they would be kind if they could but some circumstance in their lives is making that hard for them.

Whether or not their actions or words deserve compassion does not matter. You are choosing compassion because it is the best way for you to respond. It increases your joy, gives you control over yourself, and makes you more like Jesus. All those things make you happier and more successful. Why let someone else provoke negative thoughts that poison your life when you can choose better?

When something happens that causes negative thoughts to pop into your mind, stop and ask yourself a few questions: *Will feeling this way help me? Will it create joy in my life? Will it make the situation any better?* The answer to these questions is obviously no, so choose better.

While I (Lyn) waited in line at the computer store one day, the man in front of me started to get frustrated. He began yelling at the guy behind the counter, who was trying to be helpful. The salesman listened patiently and kept responding with kindness even as the man continued to be rude. When the customer finally left, I told the salesman I was impressed with how well he had handled the situation. He smiled and said, "I knew that wasn't about me. That man had a bad day or something. I get that. He just needed someone to listen and be nice to him."

The salesman had it figured out. He let the man dump his emotional junk all over while keeping his thoughts, feelings, and words positive. In the process, he kept his joy, he was a blessing to the other man, and he impressed another customer. Smart guy!

When you change the way you see things, your feelings and responses will follow. Remember, when you give someone the benefit of the doubt and respond with compassion, it actually benefits you.

LIVE 4:8 :::::::::::::::::::::::::::::::::

Work It

On the following page, write the names of the four most important people in your life in the boxes on the left. To the right, briefly describe one way you could show more compassion to each person.

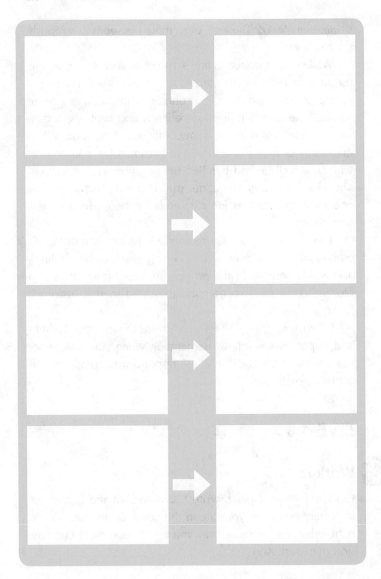

Talk It

Pick one of the four people you listed, and make him or her the target of your joy for one day. Ask God to help you think of ways to show kindness. Don't tell the person what you are doing—just do it. If you are going through this book with your youth group, a school group, or a small group, be ready to tell them what you did and how the person responded.

Stick It: Thought of the Day

My compassion protects my joy.

 ## Pray It

Lord, thank you for having compassion toward me. Please fill me today with your compassion so I can show it to others. Amen.

WE ARE SPONGES

The Joy of Our Surroundings

Above all else, guard your heart, for everything you do flows from it.
PROVERBS 4:23, NIV

YOU SOAK UP what is around you like a sponge soaks up water. You breathe. You live. You think. You walk. You talk. You go to school. You go to the mall. And as you do, you absorb the things you see and hear. What you let into your heart affects your beliefs, feelings, goals, and behaviors. Nothing comes out of your heart that you have not put there first. Remember the saying from Oklahoma we referred to on Day 7? "What's down in the well comes up in the bucket."

The best way to improve your life is to improve your thinking. And the best way to improve your thinking is to keep careful watch over your heart. When you guard your heart, you are protecting your joy. Like a computer, you are protecting your mental software from viruses. You are not letting anything in that will damage who you are. Guarding your heart is also like wearing protective glasses that shield your eyes from things that will hurt you and instead allow you to see only what is true, pure, lovely, and excellent.

Think of all the things that are protected: our president, homes, money, children, pets, and even cars. How much more important that we protect our hearts!

Many Christians do not pay much attention to what is around them. They listen to whatever is on the radio. They watch what is popular on TV. They go to the same movies everyone else is going to. They read trendy books. They listen to random conversations all day. They watch videos their friends suggest without considering ahead of time whether or not they should. Every day they are absorbing things that steal their joy and fill their minds with negative thoughts.

Instead of carefully guarding their hearts and feeding their minds only good thoughts, they simply take in whatever is going on around them. You cannot do that and at the same time grow your joy and move toward God's good plans for you. Listening to crude language, hanging around kids who are disrespectful or rebellious toward their parents, watching movies with inappropriate scenes or promiscuous themes, and ingesting excessive violence through gaming will not get you closer to your goals.

A classic Dr. Seuss book follows the journey of a character trying to get to a city named Solla Sollew. Along the way he meets with all kinds of trouble, but he keeps going, determined to get to the city. When he finally arrives at the door of

Solla Sollew and puts the key into the keyhole, a little creature reaches out and slaps the key away. Surprised, he tries again— only to have the key slapped away time after time. It turns out that a creature called the Key-Slapping Slippard guards the door to the city, allowing no one in. In fact, the Key-Slapping Slippard is so persistent that the main character gives up and goes someplace else.[1] Your mind and heart need you to be a Key-Slapping Slippard. Your job is to slap away anything that should not be there.

Put good things in your heart, and good things will come out. Put junk in, and junk will come out. It is the same idea as sowing and reaping. Author James Allen wrote in his book *As a Man Thinketh,* "Good thoughts and actions can never produce bad results; bad thoughts and actions can never produce good results."

Which do you want?

LIVE 4:8 :::::::::::::::::::::::::::::::::

 ## Work It

How can you be more careful about what goes into your heart? The first step is to know what is around you. In the first box on the following page, write down some things you see and hear on a regular basis that put negative thoughts in your mind. Places you go could fit in this category too. In the second box, write down some things you see and hear that put positive thoughts in your mind.

---

1. Dr. Seuss, *I Had Trouble in Getting to Solla Sollew* (New York: Random House, 1965).

JOY-DECREASING INPUTS	JOY-PRODUCING INPUTS

Talk It

To take action against the negative influences around you, make a playlist of music that fills your mind with good things, especially things that honor God. Ask Christian friends and family for suggestions and then play positive, faith-building music as much as possible. Share your playlist with someone, and tell him or her about the decision you have made.

Stick It: Thought of the Day

 ## Pray It

Jesus, thank you for all the good influences in my life. Please guard my heart today and protect me from bad influences. Amen.

WHAT DID YOU EAT FOR DINNER LAST NIGHT?

The Joy of Quality Questions

The LORD hates evil thoughts, but kind words please him.
PROVERBS 15:26, CEV

IMAGINE YOU and your family are sitting in front of a blazing fireplace on a cold, wintry night. A spark pops out and lands on your sweater. If you let it stay there, it might burn a hole through your clothes and then burn you. But if you quickly brush it off, the spark goes out and no harm is done.

The same is true of negative thoughts. When you train yourself to recognize them quickly, you can brush them away without any trouble.

By now you know that Philippians 4:8 is about focusing on the good stuff. But since your life is full of both positive and negative things, how do you keep your thoughts on the good stuff? How do you brush away the negative sparks that can steal your joy? How do you focus on the good stuff instead of the bad stuff?

What did you eat for dinner last night?

That's a strange question to ask right now, isn't it? What does it have to do with sparks and thoughts? Nothing. It simply was a way to get you to shift your attention to a different topic. I want you to see how easy it is to exchange one thought for another. All you have to do is ask a question.

To exchange negative thoughts for positive thoughts, you need to ask positive questions. For example, if I ask you what classes you don't like at school, you will tell me negative things. But if I ask you what classes you like the most, you will give me a positive response. Answers are often determined by the way a question is asked. You wouldn't tell me good things if I asked you, "What stinks about your neighborhood?" or "What bugs you about your sister?" or "What do your parents do to make your life miserable?"

Thinking involves asking and answering questions in your head. It is an inner conversation that goes on all day. The kinds of questions you are in the habit of asking yourself are very important. The questions you ask affect what you focus on and how you feel. They are the best way to redirect your attention from negative to positive.

Good questions are ones that require a positive answer. Here are some examples:

- What are four things I am thankful for right now?
- What are four of my favorite foods?
- Who are four people who love me?

Each one of those questions will have happy answers, and asking for four responses causes you to think about positive things longer.

Use these kinds of questions during the day. You can start your day with a positive question, ask yourself another one at lunchtime, and ask a third before you go to bed. This exercise will begin to change the way you think—and you now know that what you think determines how you live. When you ask yourself positive questions, you will think positively and live joyfully.

Like a spark on your sweater, a negative thought can be brushed away and do no harm. One negative thought does not change your joy. The negative thoughts that you let stay in your mind and burn holes there are the ones that make you unhappy, discouraged, and frustrated. Brush negative thoughts away with positive questions.

LIVE 4:8 :::::::::::::::::::::::::::::::::::

Work It

In the space provided, write four positive questions that involve three to four answers each. You can use the three questions I gave you as examples and come up with one more of your own, or you can create all new ones. Now write each question on a separate sticky note or note card. Place them where you will see them at different times of the day, such as right by your bed, on your bathroom mirror, in the car, or in your backpack.

_____

_____

_____

_____

_____

_____

_____

_____

_____

_____

_____

_____

_____

_____

_____

_____

_____

Talk It

Throughout the day, answer the questions you wrote. Repeating the same questions every day for a while will help you start the habit of thinking about the good things in your life. Share at least one of your questions and answers with someone today.

Stick It: Thought of the Day

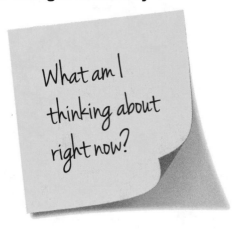

What am I thinking about right now?

 ## Pray It

Heavenly Father, thank you for the power to change my thoughts.
Today, help me to focus my mind on what is good and right. Amen.

JUST DO IT!

The Joy of Excellent Work

Whether you eat or drink, or whatever you do,
do all to the glory of God.
1 CORINTHIANS 10:31, NKJV

BY NOW, you know that God wants you to be filled with joy. But is it possible to be joy-filled all the time? Can you have joy at school or sweating through basketball or soccer practice? What about if you have a job? Can you have joy mowing lawns, babysitting, or working weekends as the cashier at Chick-fil-A? How about chores at home? Is there joy in cleaning your room, dusting, taking out the trash, or washing Dad's car? Some people go through their days unhappy and complaining about school or chores. They only experience joy when they are doing something really fun. You don't have to be like that! School and work are part of God's plan for your joy.

Before you read this, take a deep breath and hang on: you will be in school, or working, or doing chores for the rest of your life. *Gasp*, right? But here is the good news: God invented work because it's good for us. In fact, even before Adam and Eve sinned, God had given Adam work to do. God tells us in Genesis 2:15 that he put Adam in the Garden of Eden to take care of it. Work is a gift from God! You can think of it as either something you *have* to do or something you *get* to do.

I (Lyn) got my first job at thirteen. Every Saturday one of my parents drove me to the home of a family in our church. The woman who lived there had an illness that kept her in bed all the time. Her husband and daughter needed help keeping the house clean, so I spent four hours on Saturdays mopping, vacuuming, and dusting. Honestly, those aren't my favorite things to do, but I got so much joy out of helping that family that I was happy to do them. God did two great things for me through that experience. First, the woman who lived there became my friend. She enjoyed talking to me while I cleaned her bedroom, and I learned a lot from her. The second thing God did for me was turn me into a lean, mean, cleaning machine. That has come in quite handy!

Your being in school or working with your hands is important to God. It is part of who he is shaping you to be. It is also teaching you to serve and to let other people see glimpses of Jesus in you. When you go to class or work for God's glory, you approach it with energy and a desire to do well. God does everything with excellence, and he wants the same for you. Excellence grows joy and leads to success.

In everything you do, do it as if God is watching—because

he is. He is cheering you on, helping you do your best, and he is ready to reward you for a job well done.

In the Bible, Paul compares how a Christ follower should live with how an athlete trains. "You've all been to the stadium and seen the athletes race. Everyone runs; one wins. Run to win. All good athletes train hard. They do it for a gold medal that tarnishes and fades. You're after one that's gold eternally. I don't know about you, but I'm running hard for the finish line. I'm giving it everything I've got. No sloppy living for me!" (1 Corinthians 9:24-26, *The Message*).

Does that describe you? It can! Making every moment the best it can be and putting your whole heart into everything you do is the way to live a life of joy.

LIVE 4:8 :::::::::::::::::::::::::::::::::

Work It

In the left-hand column on the following page, write three things you have to do regularly that don't feel fun, such as cleaning the bathroom. In the right-hand column, beside each item, write "I will do this with excellence." In the box below the columns, write "JOY" really big.

Talk It

Tell someone you can text with about one of the things you wrote in the left-hand column and your plan to do it with excellence. Then when you do that activity well, send the person a text that says, "I did it with excellence!"

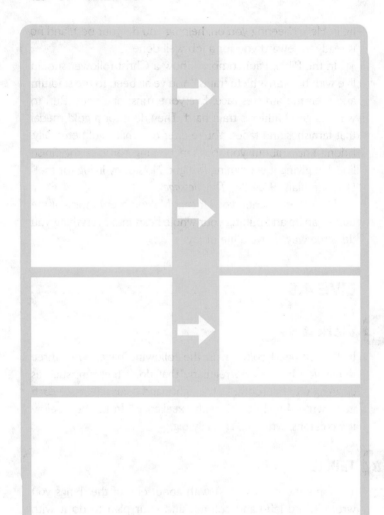

Stick It: Thought of the Day

I'm giving it everything I've got.

 Pray It

Jesus, thank you for doing everything with excellence and for giving me the power to do it too. Please help me to honor you and to increase my joy by happily doing my work to the best of my ability. Amen.

WAIT AND SEE!

The Joy of Purity

How can young people keep their lives pure? By obeying your commands.

PSALM 119:9, GNT

EVERYWHERE WE LOOK in our confused world, it's all about bodies. Advertisers use bodies to sell cars, drinks, potato chips, tools, burgers, and vacations. We get used to thinking that people are worthwhile only for what they look like. Guys and girls are valued if they are "hot" and overlooked if they're not. But the focus on bodies cheapens what God designed to be fantastic and bring us true joy.

When God made Eve, it was because Adam needed a companion. Adam had been naming the animals and had certainly noticed that there were males and females of each species, but only one of him—one human. So God gave him Eve. Their relationship began as a gift from God, not because of their looks, but because they were created to be partners.

You are not a body; you *have* a body. It is the "earth suit" God gave you for this life. What you are is a child of God. Your spirit has been sealed by the Holy Spirit as belonging to God. The light of Jesus in you shines out of your eyes and face! What is important about you is what is happening inside. Yet when you spend time reading your Bible and thinking about things that are pleasing to God, he also shows up on the outside. God says those who look to him are radiant (see Psalm 34:5). Now that's a worthwhile and attractive quality!

God knows that it is easy for us to make decisions based on what we see. In one of the Old Testament stories we read this: "The LORD told him, 'Samuel, don't think Eliab is the one [to be king] just because he's tall and handsome. He isn't the one I've chosen. People judge others by what they look like, but I judge people by what is in their hearts'" (1 Samuel 16:7, CEV). God doesn't choose people based on their appearance, and neither should you.

Placing a high value on what people look like and being distracted by it is not God's best for you. It limits the kinds of relationships you will have. Not only that, but focusing too much on people's bodies and having inappropriate sexual thoughts about them is harmful to your spiritual and emotional health. Until you are married, nobody else's body is your business. You were created with natural sexual thoughts and desires, which are wonderful because they lead to marriage. But before that time, sexual thoughts stirred up by looking at and dwelling on the wrong things are to be replaced with God thoughts. Paul says in 1 Thessalonians 4:7 that "God did not call us to be impure, but to live a holy life" (NIV).

Just as unkind, angry, or insecure thoughts steal your joy, so do impure thoughts. They focus on the wrong things, taking time and energy away from God's good plans for you. The bonus is, if you focus on other people's character, personalities, and love for God rather than just on their appearance, you will end up with the best friends . . . .and much healthier relationships!

LIVE 4:8 :::::::::::::::::::::::::::::::::

Work It

There are several ways to tackle impure thoughts: you can memorize a verse to get your thoughts going the right way. You can sing a favorite song to distract you. You can do an activity that keeps you busy and requires concentration. You can pray and ask God to help you think about something else. In the space provided, write down two positive things you will do to replace your impure thoughts.

The verse for today is a great one to memorize: "How can young people keep their lives pure? By obeying your commands" (Psalm 119:9, GNT).

_____

_____

_____

_____

_____

_____

Talk It

Write "Lovely, Pure, True!" on a sticky note to remind yourself all day that impure thoughts are not right and need to be replaced. Share the note with someone you can trust.

Stick It: Thought of the Day

I value who people are, not what they look like.

Pray It

God, thank you for giving us bodies to live in. Please help me to see people for who they are, not for what they look like. Nudge me to keep my thoughts on what is good and right. Amen.

STOP AND DROP

The Joy of Restraint

Those who are dominated by the sinful nature think about sinful things, but those who are controlled by the Holy Spirit think about things that please the Spirit. So letting your sinful nature control your mind leads to death. But letting the Spirit control your mind leads to life and peace.

ROMANS 8:5-6, NLT

JUST DROP IT!

In every moment, you are trending toward either positive, happy thoughts or negative, discouraging thoughts. You are rarely emotionally neutral but are going in one direction or the other. When you start down the negative path, you have a decision to make. You can keep going with more and more critical, sad, or discouraging thoughts until you are in a funk, or you can stop those thoughts and change direction.

You can refuse to wallow in negative thoughts. As soon as you realize the way your thoughts are going, you can stop them. When you allow them to continue, you are choosing unhappiness, which takes you off God's path of success. To get back on, start thinking positive thoughts again.

You already know how to do this. You do it all the time without even realizing it! Have you ever gotten bored during class (is that a stupid question?) and been doodling on your paper or staring out the window when your teacher called on you? Your mind immediately stopped what it was thinking about and scrambled for an answer to the teacher's question. You quit daydreaming and switched to thinking about your class.

Or imagine being in the car at night, talking with your dad as you head home. Suddenly a dog runs across the street right in front of your car, and your dad hits the brakes hard. You don't keep right on talking through that; you both stop the conversation and focus on the dog in the road. Your mind quickly makes the adjustment. It knows how to stop and drop. Part of growing up is training your mind to stop and drop when you want it to, not just when it is forced to.

You may sometimes think you're entitled to negative thoughts. Because of the way you were treated or an unpleasant situation you encountered, you feel you have the right to think critically. But even if you have the right, why would you? It doesn't help you at all. Nothing good comes from negative thinking. You can drop those thoughts any time you choose. They aren't glued to you. They aren't permanent. They can be changed at any moment.

Imagine you study really hard for a test but get a lower

grade on it than you wanted. Your first thought when seeing your test will probably be disappointment. You might say to yourself, "I can't believe it! I studied for this stupid test! This stinks." Or you might get mad at the teacher and think unkind things about her. Your first reaction is understandable, but then you have a choice. Either you can make yourself more unhappy by criticizing and complaining, or you can do something positive. You can go to your teacher, tell her you are disappointed, and ask how you can improve your grade the next time. Or you can ask a friend to study with you for the next test. You can see a low grade as failure or as motivation to do better.

By catching negative thoughts early and choosing positive thoughts instead, you can solve problems, enjoy happier relationships, keep yourself on God's path of success, and experience more joy.

LIVE 4:8 :::::::::::::::::::::::::::::::::::

Work It

Take a few moments to think about the difference between keeping and dropping negative thoughts. On the next page, list the reasons for keeping negative thoughts in the left-hand column. In the other column, list the reasons for dropping them.

Talk It

Get a piece of string or yarn or a loose-fitting rubber band and put it around your wrist. Every time you look at it, let it remind you to drop negative thoughts and choose positive ones instead. Explain its purpose to one person today.

KEEPING THE NEGATIVE	DROPPING THE NEGATIVE

 Stick It: Thought of the Day

I stop and drop negative thoughts.

 Pray It

Heavenly Father, thank you for giving my mind the ability to stop and drop negative thoughts. Please help me to do that all day today and fill my mind with positive thoughts. Amen.

DON'T SWEAT THE BIG STUFF

The Joy of Conquering

Dear brothers and sisters, when troubles of any kind come your way, consider it an opportunity for great joy. For you know that when your faith is tested, your endurance has a chance to grow.

JAMES 1:2-3, NLT

TROUBLES ARE GOOD for you. That sounds impossible, but it's true. Troubles are what shape your character. And trying to avoid difficulties is like trying to avoid life. If you are somehow able to stay away from problems, you probably live in a cave.

With God's help, though, troubles don't need to make you nervous or get you upset. It may take a little practice, but you can be joyful even in the middle of hard things. When you remain calm and peaceful during difficulties, you do a much better job of handling them, whatever they may be.

The negative, scary, frustrating feelings you can have during difficult times make you feel out of control. It's like racing downhill on a bike with no handles and no brakes. Sometimes that out-of-control feeling comes because of external circumstances in our lives, like being overwhelmed with schoolwork or dealing with a tough relationship. Other times it comes because of our own choices. For example, you may feel out of control when you know you're not doing what the Bible says or when you aren't close to God.

But if you never had tough times, you would never appreciate the good times. God uses hard stuff to grow good things in you. Obstacles develop your character, just as lifting weights develops your muscles. Neither one is much fun when you are in the middle of it, but both produce great results.

Weight training is good for your body and makes you look and feel better. It makes you stronger and healthier. Just as your physical muscles become stronger when they resist weight, so do the "muscles" in your mind, spirit, and character.

Character is grown through problems, but strong character depends on how you choose to respond. Things that frustrate you or cause you to struggle can make you into someone exceptional—or someone defeated. It is what you learn from trouble that grows your character to be like Jesus.

Your character is the expression of who you are. It is the total of your thoughts and habits, both the good and the bad. Character isn't something you are born with; it is something that grows throughout your life and with every choice you make. You never quite know what you are made of until you are squeezed. Then what comes out shows what you have been putting in and what you have been thinking about. When you are in a tough spot, how do you respond? What do your reactions say about your character?

Trouble comes in all shapes and sizes. It can be relationships, injuries, unmet needs, disappointments, and even the weather. Trouble doesn't play favorites; it strikes everyone at one time or another.

Consider for a moment that the biggest problem you have might be exactly what is needed to grow your character so that you become perfectly prepared to follow God's path for your life. Seeing trouble as a character-builder takes away its power. It can't hurt you when you see it as potentially good. The truth is, when you feel the stress of problems, growth is trying to happen. Looking at difficulties as natural, normal, and even necessary gives you the ability to use them for your good.

What happens when you are being squeezed by a hard situation? How do you handle a best friend's betrayal? What about that teacher you don't get along with? How do you respond to the coach who yells at you or keeps you on the bench? What do you say or do when your parents don't give you what you want, or when there's tension in your home? Troubles can be turned into good when you trust God to be bigger, stronger, and tougher than anything you face.

You can find treasure in the trouble, but you must train yourself to look for it! New challenges can either defeat you or inspire you. They will either tear you down or build you up. Decide, with God's help, to change all your problems into your good and for God's glory. Don't sweat the big stuff. God is in control, and he's got you covered!

LIVE 4:8 ::::::::::::::::::::::::::::::::::

Work It

List any big troubles in your life right now. Across from each trouble write, "Good for me." In the box at the bottom write, "Covered by God."

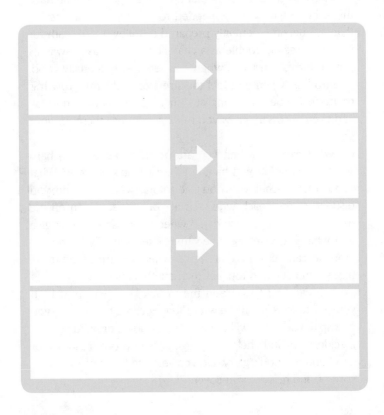

Talk It

Write Psalm 18:29 on a card or sticky note: "In your strength I can crush an army; with my God I can scale any wall" (NLT). Share with someone how God is growing and strengthening you through your troubles.

Stick It: Thought of the Day

With God, I'll get through this!

Pray It

Jesus, thank you for being with me, especially in troubles. Today, please show me what you want me to learn and how you want me to grow in both the good things and the bad. Amen.

NO EXCUSES

The Joy of Owning It

Who may worship in your sanctuary, LORD? Who may enter your presence on your holy hill? Those who lead blameless lives and do what is right, speaking the truth from sincere hearts.
PSALM 15:1-2, NLT

A COMEDY CAME OUT a few years ago about a guy who accidentally went into outer space. All kinds of crazy events transpired and he did a lot of silly things, but every time something happened that could get him in trouble, he would say, "It wasn't me"—even if it *was* his fault. The movie tried to make that funny, but in real life, lying or making excuses isn't funny. It also isn't good for us.

Your ability to take ownership of yourself—both what you

do and the results of those choices—will determine your reputation, your success, and the amount of joy in your life.

When you make excuses for something that went wrong—or, worse, try to blame someone else—people learn not to trust you. Most of the time excuses sound lame, which makes it seem like you are lying. And when you blame someone else, that person feels betrayed, and it makes you look selfish and unkind. Making excuses and blaming doesn't work, and they aren't worth it.

Taking responsibility in the little things of life means people—and, more important, God—can trust you to be responsible with bigger things. If you want to be trusted to get a good job, to be elected president of the student council, or to be captain of the volleyball team, you have to own your behavior. You have to be willing to step up and say, "I am responsible. That was my fault."

Owning your behavior means not making excuses for a mistake. For example, imagine you have a week to get a project done, but you wait until the night before to start working on it. It turns out to be more complicated than you thought it would be, so you have to hurry, and you don't do a very good job. When you get a poor grade on the project and your parents or teacher ask you what happened, you have a choice. You can make up an excuse, such as, "The library didn't have the books I needed until the end of the week" or "I misunderstood the instructions and had to redo it at the last minute," or you can take ownership of your mistake and admit that you waited too long to start working on the project.

Saying those words out loud may be embarrassing, but it will deepen the respect your parents or teacher have for you. They know how hard it is to admit a mistake, and when you do, they see your integrity. Being known as a trustworthy person is extremely important. Look at what God says about it: "A good reputation and respect are worth much more than silver and gold" (Proverbs 22:1, CEV).

At times it may feel that making an excuse or blaming someone else will get you out of a jam. That is not true! You may have temporary success, but your actions will catch up with you. You will feel guilty for having done the wrong thing, you will lose your joy, and you will eventually have to apologize and ask forgiveness. Why not do it right in the first place? God always blesses right choices.

Watch the little things. If you are late because it took you too long to get ready, don't blame the traffic. If you simply don't want to go somewhere, don't say it's because you don't feel well. If your little brother tries to hand you the phone and it's someone you don't want to talk to, don't say, "Tell him I'm not here." Everything you say needs to be true. That's taking ownership. It gives you a clear conscience and lots of joy.

LIVE 4:8 ::::::::::::::::::::::::::::::::::::

Work It

On the following page, write down times or situations where you tend to make excuses. In the box at the bottom of the page, write, "I don't make excuses. I own my behavior."

1

2

3

Talk It

If you recently made an excuse for something or blamed some-one else, it is not too late to make it right. It's never too late to do the right thing! Go to that person, explain what you did or said, ask for forgiveness, and do whatever it takes to fix the situation. Then share your experience of taking ownership with someone else.

 ## Stick It: Thought of the Day

I tell
the truth.

 ## Pray It

Father God, thank you for showing me where I am not truthful and where I am not taking responsibility for my choices. Please fill my heart and words with truth. Help me to be a person of integrity. Amen.

WAY TO GO!

The Joy of Other People's Success

Speak encouraging words to one another. Build up hope so you'll all be together in this, no one left out, no one left behind.
1 THESSALONIANS 5:11, *THE MESSAGE*

GOD WANTS EVERY ONE of his children to succeed at what he created them to do. He wants us to reach our potential and to have an impact on the world. As each of us succeeds in various ways, our successes benefit others. The success of one doesn't threaten the success of another. Just because one person receives a huge blessing doesn't mean there's not enough left for you or me. God's resources are endless! There is plenty to go around.

The truth is that everyone can fulfill his or her potential

without cheating anyone else in the process. God's success system makes room for everyone to do well.

For Christ followers, success is learning to make God's desires our desires. Success means every day becoming a little bit more like the person we were created to be. Ultimately, it means becoming more and more like Jesus. Then every success we experience will shine his light onto others and benefit their lives in countless ways. Success is to be celebrated and shared.

Imagine that an outstanding basketball player comes to your school. He's tall and strong, and he can shoot consistently from the three-point line. His skill and good attitude energize the whole team. Pretty soon, they are winning games. The bleachers start filling with people who cheer the team on to greater success. During games, more popcorn is sold, bringing in more money for the band program. A student artist is asked to design a special T-shirt for students to wear on game days. The sale of the shirts supports the art and drama clubs. The community gets excited and starts offering sales on their products on game days. Restaurants offer discounts for people who eat there after games. Everyone is benefiting and enjoying the success of the team.

When we get excited about others' success, and when we can join in and help them, we get to experience all the fun. Serving others on their way to success creates blessing for them, for you, and for more people. God wants us to cheer each other on in the things we do well. Choose to become the biggest cheerleader for your best friend, your brother or sister (yes, especially them!), your youth leader, and your parents.

People succeed in all kinds of ways. It is easy to find things to cheer for in other people's lives. Maybe it's a friend who writes a winning essay, wins the spelling bee, scores the final touch-down, or tries something for the first time that he or she has been afraid of. Be the one who says, "Wow, you're awesome!" Send texts, tweets, or Facebook notes of congratulations.

Too many people drag others down with their bad attitudes and jealousy. Trying to pour cold water on someone's success or talking smack about him or her mainly hurts the one doing it. Resenting someone for doing well steals *your* joy, not his or hers. Instead, be better than that. Celebrate good stuff! We need people who serve, give, create, grow, and lead. There is plenty of opportunity to go around.

If you are secure in God's love, you know that he has a plan for you that isn't threatened by anyone else's talent or success. Be happy for what he is doing through others, and know that he is working through your life, too. Think and speak positive things about other people when they succeed and you'll be filled with even more joy.

And if you're the one succeeding, be kind to others in the process.

LIVE 4:8 :::::::::::::::::::::::::::::::::::

 ## Work It

Think of three successful people. On the following page, next to each name, write what you admire about them. In the third column, list the people who have benefited from their success.

154 // THINK 4:8

PERSON	CHARACTERISTICS	BENEFICIARIES

Talk It

Think of two or three people you know who are working really hard on something. Take a few moments to pray for their success. Ask God to help them achieve what they are trying to do. Today, text or write them words of encouragement, or call and tell them you are cheering them on.

 Stick It: Thought of the Day

I have joy when others do well.

 Pray It

Jesus, thank you for other people's success. Please help me today to celebrate the cool things you are doing through others. Amen.

CONSTRUCTION ZONE

The Joy of Agreeing with God

Words kill, words give life; they're either poison or fruit—you choose.
PROVERBS 18:21, *THE MESSAGE*

WHEN MY KIDS were little, I (Lyn) spent hours building block towers with them. We had big cardboard blocks that we could stack quite high. Building the towers was fun, but the real excitement came when it was time to knock them down. Sometimes my kids would get a running start and throw themselves into the blocks, while other times, they would just start flailing their arms into the tower and laugh as it tumbled down.

Knocking down what we built was tons of fun when we were little, but unfortunately, as we get older, we sometimes knock down more important things. When we start experiencing some success, we wreck our own progress by telling ourselves we'll never make it, or by being afraid or lazy. We get in our own way! We need to stop tearing ourselves down and start building ourselves up. One of the best ways to do that is to affirm what is true. *Affirm* means to agree, so affirming what is true means agreeing with God about who we are and his good plans for us.

Affirmations are like positive mental vitamins. They put good, right, healthy thoughts in your mind, which then produce good, right, healthy actions. The words you say to yourself are like seeds that, once planted, begin to shape your life and how you see the world. The truth is, you are always affirming something because you are always thinking. You are either agreeing with good things or agreeing with bad things. You are either building yourself up or tearing yourself down with every thought.

There are two questions to ask yourself: *First, what are you affirming? Second, would you be affirming the same things if Jesus were physically standing next to you?*

Most of us let random negative thoughts tear us down without realizing that's what we've done. One minute you might be thanking God for how much he loves you, and the next minute you're feeling rejected because someone said something mean. You feel confident in your good grades until you mess up a test and suddenly feel like a failure. We constantly go back and forth between positive and negative.

Imagine getting in the car to go to a game with some friends. You're almost there when the driver turns around and heads back to your house. You say, "I thought we were going to the game," so he makes his way back toward the game. When you're almost there, he changes direction *again* and drives back toward your house. Going back and forth doesn't make sense, right?

We are often like that driver when it comes to our thoughts. We think good things and focus on what is going well, only to have a negative thought slam in and change our direction. We become unhappy and discouraged in seconds. It doesn't have to be this way!

When we affirm God's goodness, we are focusing on his love, his blessings, and his joy. We're remembering what he says about us—that we are his beloved children and his masterpieces—and holding on to that as the most important thing in our lives. Refuse to affirm, or agree with, anything that you don't want in your life. Don't take ownership of negative things by saying *my* cold, *my* headache, *my* awful teacher, *my* low grade, *my* lack of money, *my* lost ring, or *my* troubled friendship. Instead, take a mental vitamin and attach your thoughts to what you do want, such as joy, fun, good grades, and healthy relationships.

As much as it's possible, stay out of conversations that criticize others or express negative attitudes. Those words are contagious and easily become your thoughts. Just as you turn your head away when someone sneezes right next to you, turn away from negative words and attitudes around you.

Be aware of your words—the ones you say to others and the ones you say to yourself. Build up what you want in your life based on God's promises and his good plans for you. Being positive also makes you more aware of the blessings God has already given you, and that adds to your joy.

LIVE 4:8 :::

Work It

Write four good, right, healthy thoughts that affirm God's goodness.

* _____

_____

_____

* _____

_____

_____

* _____

_____

_____

* _____

_____

_____

Talk It

Below are four of God's promises. Choose one to write on a card or piece of paper to carry with you, or input it into your phone. Read it regularly to keep your thoughts on what builds good things in your life.

God can do more than I ask or imagine. (See Ephesians 3:20.)

Those who seek God lack no good thing. (See Psalm 34:10.)

Nothing can ever separate us from the love of God. (See Romans 8:38-39.)

Jesus will be with us always. (See Matthew 28:20.)

 ## Stick It: Thought of the Day

I am a builder!

 ## Pray It

Lord, thank you for filling my life with good things. Please help me today to affirm your goodness with my thoughts, words, and actions. Amen.

MOTION RULES EMOTION

The Joy of Self-Discipline

If anyone obeys his word, God's love is truly made complete in him.
1 JOHN 2:5, NIV

NOBODY REALLY LIKES the idea of discipline, but self-discipline is actually a very good thing. It takes all the best parts of your life—such as your talent, your interests, your health, and your relationships—and points them in the right direction. Self-discipline kicks in when you feel like a loser or when you're just in a bad mood. It stops you before you go too far down the path of self-pity and says, "Oh no, you don't! You are better than this."

People who are undisciplined give in to their feelings, which squashes joy and causes all sorts of trouble. What happens when you live by your emotions? You do only the things you *feel* like doing. Whatever you feel at any moment becomes what guides you. Yet if you do your homework only when you feel like it, you will probably flunk out of school. If you consume only junk food because that's what you feel like eating, you will eventually become unhealthy. If your mom does things for you only when she feels like it, your life will change a lot . . . and, I assure you, not in a good way!

Making yourself do things that are good and right even when you don't feel like it opens your life up to success and joy. There is a huge difference between what you can't do to improve your life and what you won't do. *Can't* is about real inability or restrictions, but *won't* is a choice based on feelings. Lots of people toss their bad habits in the "can't do anything about that" pile when they really belong in the "won't do anything about that" pile. That behavior lessens the good things in life. You don't have to live like that.

Some kids say they don't have any friends at school or youth group. They have accepted the situation as something they can't change, whereas in many cases it's something they won't change. They normally might walk into a room and sit down by themselves. They don't approach other people and start conversations, and they don't go to activities or get involved with the kids who are happy and active. Rather than making an effort to change the situation, they act helpless, as if they have no control over it. Sure, some people are naturally more extroverted than others, but everyone can make an effort to be friendly.

You can control how you feel, the decisions you make, and the way you behave. That's good news! You can make decisions based on what you want for your life and what's right rather than on how you feel.

You can actually act your way into the feelings you ultimately want. As long as your goals line up with God's Word, he will help you reach them. For example, if you want more joy or if you want to be a more loving person, begin to behave more joyfully and more lovingly. Over time, as you put those good goals into action, they will become a real part of your identity. Imagine reaching your greatest goal or having your biggest prayer answered, and live out those feelings. They're the feelings you will have when God answers your prayers and you achieve your goals, so start making them real now. You can choose them by disciplining your mind and your mood.

God has given you this power to encourage personal change, even though it may not feel comfortable at first. Any new behavior feels a little strange until you get used to it. You can sit around and wait for your feelings to get you moving, or you can take action and expect the feelings to follow. After all, the word *emotion* is 86 percent *motion*.

When you choose actions that please God, he will give you the feelings you desire. And when you follow what God says even if you don't feel like it, you will begin to experience the joy that comes from pleasing the one who made you and knows you so well.

LIVE 4:8 :

Work It

As you have just read, what you do can have a dramatic effect on how you feel. In the three boxes on the left, write three ways you want to feel, such as confident, calm, or happy. In the boxes on the right, write a God-pleasing activity that helps you feel that way.

Talk It

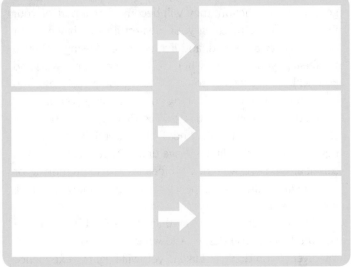

Find someone who will do one of those activities with you. Tell him or her that you're doing the activity in order to create certain feelings. You are learning and proving that you can act your way into a feeling. You are in control of how you feel!

Stick It: Thought of the Day

I take charge of my feelings.

 Pray It

Heavenly Father, thank you for giving me the courage and discipline to do what you want me to do, whether or not I feel like it. Amen.

ROCK IT!

The Joy of Using Your Strengths

We are God's masterpiece. He has created us anew in Christ Jesus, so we can do the good things he planned for us long ago.
EPHESIANS 2:10, NLT

YOU ARE GOOD at certain stuff for a reason. God made you that way so you can fulfill his purpose joyfully.

The flip side is that you are also lousy at a bunch of things. The lousy list will always be longer than the good list because there are lots of people in the world who are really good at whatever you are not. If you spend too much time on the lousy stuff, you will lose a bunch of joy. Doing too many things you don't excel at takes energy away from what you are good at.

Since God made us to interact with other people, he

wants us to work with each other to accomplish his will. In fact, he has created billions of people to get his job done, so there is no pressure on any of us to do the things we are not good at. Someone else can do them very well. The apostle Paul writes, "The human body has many parts, but the many parts make up one whole body. So it is with the body of Christ" (1 Corinthians 12:12, NLT). Each person has a unique role to play.

Since you're still alive, we know that God has plans for you—and his plans blow yours away. This is not a guess; it's a fact. God has a specific plan for your life, and it makes use of your gifts, talents, passions, and personality. Your areas of interest—what you enjoy doing the most—are likely where your talents and giftedness lie.

In school, some people are naturally good at math, while others are better at science or English. Teachers want you to be good at everything, and many parents do as well. After all, getting an education is intended to teach you about many different topics. In the process, however, you will discover that you like some subjects more than others. Although it is important to do your best in all your classes, pay attention to the ones that you enjoy most. When you get to college and beyond, you will be able to choose more and more to do the things that you are good at and that you enjoy.

Some people are awesome at sports, and others are fantastic at singing or painting. Some people are neat and organized and always "color inside the lines," while others have a harder time with structure and tend to be creative and expressive. You may be great at building friendships, drawing, or speaking in front of a group. There are many different talents!

When you use your special talents, your brain releases

chemicals that give you a sense of happiness and make you want to continue. My brain never reacted that way when I was doing math, but it did give me great joy when I sang, performed, taught, or spoke publicly. God was letting me know early on that he had gifted me as a communicator. Now I am a speaker and an author, and I love it!

You tend to get great joy from doing something you are good at. As a result, you practice it over and over because it makes you so happy. The more you do it, the better you get, until it becomes one of your strengths.

Your unique mix of talents, experiences, personality, and even challenges sparks a vision inside you. The more you pursue your passions and do what you love, the more you will understand what God wants for your life. Those who become great at what they love become champions who do giant things in the world.

Will you be one of them?

LIVE 4:8 :

 ## Work It

Take a few minutes to think about your strengths. On the following page, write down three of your talents or things you love to do on the left side. Next to each one, write down on the right side what you could do in the next month to develop that strength. In the box at the bottom, list some things you can imagine doing with your life based on what you love to do now.

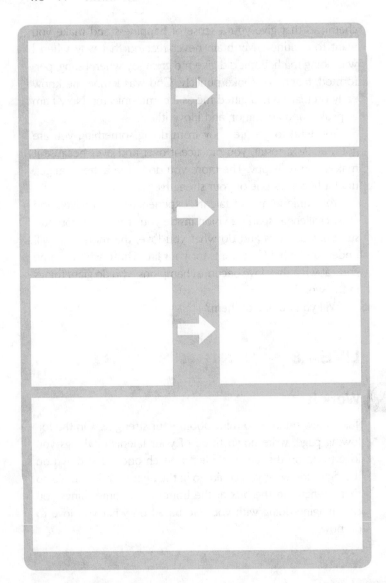

Talk It

Tell a teacher, parent, grandparent, or youth leader what you love to do and what you believe your talents are. Ask for suggestions of what you could do with those talents when you are an adult. Write the answers down someplace you can see them, and talk to God about them often.

Stick It: Thought of the Day

I have God-given strengths, and I'm using them today!

Pray It

God, thank you for creating me with special talents that you will use in amazing ways. Please help me to take my talents seriously and work hard at being the best I can be. May my life bring you glory! Amen.

SUPERSIZE YOUR FRUIT

The Joy of Living for Jesus

My old self has been crucified with Christ. It is no longer I who live, but Christ lives in me. So I live in this earthly body by trusting in the Son of God, who loved me and gave himself for me.

GALATIANS 2:20, NLT

WHEN BABIES ARE BORN, as precious as they are, they are little bundles of need. (Thankfully, God gives parents joy in meeting their children's needs!) Babies need to be fed, they need to be held, they need to be bathed, they need to sleep, and they need to have their diapers changed. They cannot meet any of their needs on their own; they are completely dependent. As they grow into toddlers and preschoolers, their needs continue to be met by other people, so they naturally think that everything is about them and what they want. Young children are by nature totally self-centered.

As we grow up, we begin to figure out that not everyone will do what we want. We learn to think about what other people might need, and we discover that doing things for others makes them happy and brings us joy. The process of becoming less selfish and self-absorbed is a good one. Being concerned about others is an attractive quality and one that can bring some success.

There is an extra part of this process for Christians, however, and this one point can have huge results in your life. It's the secret reason for most of the joy you see in other Christ followers and for the successes they experience. Every one of us can have it, but not all of us choose it. I'm talking about choosing to live for Jesus.

Jesus told a story about a farmer who threw seeds onto four different kinds of soil. Three kinds were not good for growing, so the seeds did not thrive. The fourth kind of soil was healthy enough for the seeds to grow, but not all the seeds produced the same amount of fruit. Picture it this way: some seeds grew thirty pieces of fruit, others grew sixty, and still others grew one hundred.

As a believer, you can influence the quantity and quality of your fruit. How much do you want to love Jesus and live for him? How much joy and success do you desire? All followers of Christ produce some fruit—a service or something of value that glorifies God—but the amount is up to each person. The less you live for yourself and the more you live for Jesus, the more fruit your life will produce. And of course, the more fruit you produce for Jesus, the more joy and success you will experience. Who wouldn't want that?

Living for Jesus means thinking more about him than about yourself. It means wanting other people to see not just you, but him in you. It means asking him to give you his desires so that you want what he wants. It means thinking and saying things that are true, honorable, right, pure, lovely, admirable, excellent, and worthy of praise. It means living out Philippians 4:8 so that Jesus shines through you. It is believing that what God has planned for you is better than anything you can come up with on your own.

You can be halfhearted about your relationship with Jesus, but then your whole life will be halfhearted. God created you to be the most fulfilled and joyful when you are full of him! Anything less is just okay. Why settle for okay when you can be great?

Everyone lives for something: themselves, someone they love, popularity, wealth, power, the chance to perform, to create, to be desired . . . or Jesus. Only one of those options can't fail and is, in fact, guaranteed to bring you the most joy.

LIVE 4:8 :::::::::::::::::::::::::::::::::::

Work It

Being a genuine Christ follower requires three simple things. If these are in place, God takes care of the rest. How badly do you want to live for God? Read these three statements and circle your commitment:

I will live for Jesus every day.   *Yes*   *No*

I will read something in my Bible every day.   *Yes*   *No*

I will talk to God every day.   *Yes*   *No*

If you don't know what to read in your Bible, you can start by reading a psalm or part of a psalm every day. Some people like to start in the book of John. The main thing is to get started. God will speak to your mind and heart no matter what part of the Bible you read.

Talk It

When you make a commitment or decision of any kind, you are more likely to follow through if you tell someone else. Share the commitments you just made with a person you trust.

Stick It: Thought of the Day

I live for Jesus!

Pray It

Jesus, I want to live my life for you, not for me. Help me to do what I have committed to do and to experience your awesome joy and success. Amen.

THE MASTER'S MIND

The Joy of His Thoughts

Think the same way that Christ Jesus thought.
PHILIPPIANS 2:5, CEV

YOU DON'T NEED any help to think like most people do.

Without anyone's encouraging you to think differently, you will naturally think about what is wrong with your life and what is messed up in the world. Sadly, this typical way of thinking causes most people to miss the fun and peace that coincide with a joy-filled life.

The great news for you and me is that we have a choice! Every moment is a new beginning and a fresh opportunity to become who God wants you to be. He gives you the ability to change yourself anytime you want. Your thoughts can become different, changing your character and recharging your life. God wants you to be completely alive and bursting with joy. After all, you are his child. Would he want anything less for you?

You can become everything God had in mind when he created you. No matter what you've done in the past or what your situation is now, your future can go way beyond even your wildest dreams. There is only one catch: you must learn to think like God thinks!

You may be wondering, *How can I do that? He's God!* Well, of course you can't literally think like God does, because he knows everything, is everywhere, and can do anything. But you can learn to focus your thoughts on whatever shows God's character and heart.

To understand how God thinks, you first need to know who God is. If you were to take a quick look through the Bible, you would see these truths about God:

- God is love.
- God is all-powerful.
- God is always present.
- God is all-knowing.
- God is absolute truth.
- God is holy.
- God is caring.
- God is faithful.
- God is just.
- God is unchanging.

This is a short list compared to all the things the Bible tells us about our creator, but it is enough to help you on your journey to thinking like God.

Jeremiah 17:9 tells us that "the human heart is the most deceitful of all things" (NLT), and that means we desperately need God's help to think like he does. Your heart needs to become more like God's so that your mind can become more like his. Changing your heart and your mind comes from reading the Bible and talking to God, as we discussed in Day 33. As you grow to know him better, you will find your character becoming like his. You'll begin to care about the things he cares about. Your opinions and perspectives will change, and so may some of your dreams for the future. Because you'll be living more closely to the way you were designed to live, you'll experience more joy.

God wants to place his character and power in every one of his children. When you let him do that in you, your life will change—sometimes dramatically, but more often gradually. And your positive influence will even spur productive change in the people around you.

LIVE 4:8 :::::::::::::::::::::::::::::::::

Work It

On the following page, pick an area such as school, friends, family life, or sports, and identify where your thinking and attitude might conflict with God's best for you. Then pinpoint some positive examples in your life where your thinking already lines up with God's best. Finally, select one area, such as academics or your relationship with your parents, where you can upgrade your thinking over the next forty days using Philippians 4:8 as your guide.

Talk It

Write, "What Would Jesus Think?" (WWJT) on a sticky note or a card and carry it with you all day. If you sense your thoughts getting locked on unhelpful thoughts, use this question to steer them in a more productive direction. Share the question with someone, and explain how or why you are using it.

Stick It: Thought of the Day

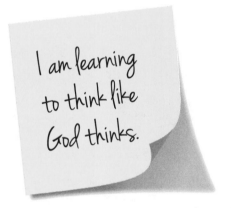

I am learning to think like God thinks.

Pray It

Lord, thank you for who you are and for giving me the power to think like you do. Please help me to focus on Philippians 4:8 Thoughts. Amen.

GOD IS CHEERING
YOU ON

The Joy of Discovery

You will seek me and find me when you seek me with all your heart.
JEREMIAH 29:13, NIV

MY CITY HOLDS a yearly event that I (Lyn), along with thousands of other people, attend. At this event several years ago, I bought something and carried it in a bag for the rest of the day. At some point, as I switched the bag from one hand to the other, a ring that is very special to me slipped off my finger. It wasn't until hours later as I was getting into my car that I realized the ring was gone.

I felt sick! I looked back at all the buildings and walkways where my ring could be and knew it was hopeless. All those feet stepping on it or kicking it—I would never find it. But because that ring meant so much to me, I took a deep breath and headed back.

As I walked, I asked God to help me find the ring. On my own, it would have been impossible, but I knew God could lead me right to it if he wanted to. Retracing my steps the best I could, my eyes scanned the grass and walkways looking for a tiny, silver circle. In less than ten minutes, I spotted it on the ground—with shoes walking all around it. Somehow God enabled me to see that one little thing in a sea of activity. I actually screamed, said "excuse me" to the people in my way, and ran to pick up the ring. My joy exploded as I found what I had been so desperately seeking.

God made you with a unique purpose, and it's your responsibility and privilege to search for it as single-mindedly as I looked for my ring. Until you find your special place in God's plan, part of your joy will be hidden from you. Nothing will seem quite right until you are doing exactly what God created you to do.

You may get so busy keeping up with the things you need to do—homework, helping around the house, practices, church activities—that you forget about God. You forget that he has a special plan for you! The things you are doing now as a teen-ager are good and worthwhile in and of themselves, but they are also preparing you for your great life purpose. You have a divine mission that will serve others and bring you joy at the same time.

Right now, doing what your parents, teachers, coaches, and church leaders ask you to do is your greatest service. At this point in your life, you are learning a lot and growing up.

That is God's plan for you now, but don't forget that he is getting you ready for the special purpose that waits for you. Nothing will give you greater joy than knowing you are doing what God wants you to do and that you are seeking his path for your life.

One of your biggest responsibilities as a teenager and, sooner than you may realize, as a twentysomething is to figure out what God wants you to do. Ask him to help you discover his divine plan for you. Refuse to be like everyone else. Be the original, unique person God created. Accept that you have a special place in this world that is ordained by God. It's up to you to find it.

There are no extra human beings. Your true place is on your unique path to glorifying God. No one can take your place, just as you cannot take someone else's place. Each of us needs to seek God's will so that we live the joyous, awesome life he planned for us. God's plan will take some people all over the world. Another's special place might be a particular neighborhood. Every God-given purpose is valuable, no matter what it is. The point is to find yours.

What is God whispering in your heart? As you read your Bible and talk to God, he will faithfully show you what he has for you. He will guide you as you think about where to work, where to live, where to go to college, or (someday) who to marry. He wants you to be successful and experience all the joy you can! He promises that if you seek him, you will find him. He is cheering you on.

LIVE 4:8 ::

Work It

Write a short description of how you are seeking God. Then answer this question: What are you hoping to find?

_____

_____

_____

_____

_____

_____

_____

_____

Talk It

Get with a friend and take turns answering these four questions:

>Who am I?
>Why am I here?
>Where might God want me to go?
>What might God want me to do?

Stick It: Thought of the Day

I have a special place in this world.

 ## Pray It

Father God, thank you for making me unique. I trust you to show me your perfect plan for my life as I seek you. Please help me to be faithful to you every day. Amen.

MY PLEASURE!

The Joy of Cleaning Feet

Each of you should look not only to your own interests,
but also to the interests of others.

PHILIPPIANS 2:4, NIV

STARTING WHEN YOU were young, your parents have probably taught you to do things such as make your bed, hang up your clothes, put your shoes away, take out the garbage, keep the bathroom clean, and pack your lunch. We all need to learn how to take care of ourselves so that we are healthy, so that our environment is neat and organized, and so that our stuff stays in good condition. But there is another good reason to learn to do things for ourselves: so that other people don't have to do it.

Taking responsibility for yourself makes life easier for those around you. When someone else has to pick up your stuff, it uses their time and takes their energy away from other things they could be doing. Why should someone else have to clean toothpaste splatter off the bathroom mirror or take your stuff out of the car when you can easily do it yourself?

Cleaning up after yourself is a way of serving others. It shows respect for their time and respect for their value as people. They weren't placed here by God to enable you to relax! Show consideration for the people around you by taking care of yourself and your things. After all, your irresponsibility becomes someone else's unwanted responsibility, and that's uncool—and no way to spread joy.

My (Lyn's) kitchen has a long, wraparound counter that isn't far from the garage door. When we first moved to this house, we quickly became lazy. It was way too easy to walk in the back door and drop everything on the counter. Books, half-filled water bottles, lunch bags, backpacks, and jackets would stay there for days. Finally, one of us would either get frustrated with the piles of stuff and put it all away or get frustrated with the people who left it all there and let them know it! Neither of those responses was the best one.

We had to retrain ourselves to immediately put away the things that belonged in the kitchen and then go straight to our own bedrooms to put away everything else. Nobody is allowed to leave things out that someone else would have to put away. When everyone is responsible for his or her own possessions, everyone experiences more joy.

Serving others also involves thinking of how you can meet their needs or how you can bless them. If someone near you drops something, pick it up. If someone is struggling to carry too many things, offer to help. Hold the door for the person behind you. If you walk up to a restaurant counter at the same time as someone else, let them order first. If you are watching a movie at home with your family and you get up for a drink or a snack, ask if they would like some too. Train your mind to think about what you can do for other people.

Kindness, selflessness, and thoughtfulness come from Jesus. When Christ fills your life and you are thinking God thoughts, you will act like him. Many people wrongly think that serving others isn't fun or makes you look stupid. Nothing could be more wrong! Serving others brings you joy because you're doing what Jesus would do. Anytime you act like Jesus, God fills you with joy.

When Jesus lived on earth, he lived in a place with hot, dusty roads where the people wore sandals. When a guest entered a home, a servant would wash his feet. Jesus showed his followers how to serve others by washing their feet himself. Jesus—our God—washing feet! If he can serve like that, so can you. Serve with genuine joy. And when someone expresses gratitude for your efforts, respond as they do at Chick-fil-A with the simple words "My pleasure."

LIVE 4:8 :

 ## Work It

On the following page, in the box labeled "Me," write three things you can do to make life easier for those around you. In the box labeled "Others," write three things you can do to bless other people.

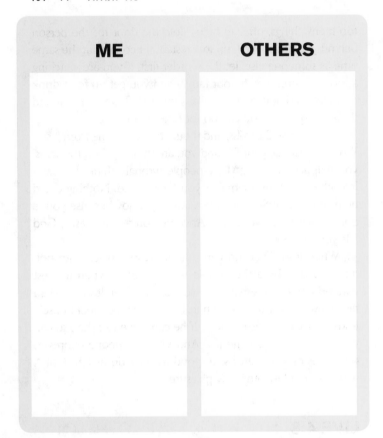

ME	OTHERS

Talk It

It's time to put those words into action. Do what you wrote! Then, at the end of the day or when you get the opportunity, share with someone how it felt to serve and bless others.

Stick It: Thought of the Day

I serve
and bless
others.

 Pray It

Jesus, thank you for showing me how to serve, and for serving me every day by taking care of me. Please help me to bless others with your kindness and thoughtfulness. Amen.

IT'S ALL IN YOUR HEAD

The Joy of Focus

You should keep a clear mind in every situation.
2 TIMOTHY 4:5, NLT

HAVE YOU EVER IMAGINED you were a superhero? I've always wondered what it would be like to fly, have X-ray vision, or show off my amazing crime-fighting skills. But the truth is, we don't need special powers to think and act our way into joy; we just need to make good use of what we already have. We have the simple power to choose what we think about all day long.

The way you think most of the time makes your life experience either junky or joyous. Focusing your thoughts, or having mental discipline, means learning to keep your mind on the right things, even when distracting thoughts are trying to push in. If you can learn to control your thoughts consistently, you will reach your goals faster, experience more joy, and become a lot more fun to be around.

Without the right thoughts, even easy things become stressful. When your mind is lazy, your feelings go up and down. Mental laziness steals your potential for greatness.

When you work to improve your thoughts, you will handle every area of your life better. Your relationships with your parents and siblings will be more peaceful. You will do your homework more quickly because you are choosing to think positively about it. The muscles of your mind will get stronger, and you will have more confidence.

This kind of focus, or mental discipline, has four elements worth considering:

Clarity: identifying what you want to do right now and what you want to do later. It's important to know what needs to be done today, such as setting your alarm so you can get up for school, taking your sports gear to practice, and getting to church on time. It's also important to think about what you want to do next year or in a few years, such as filling out college applications, sending audition tapes to drama or music schools, and graduating from high school with a strong GPA. When your "later" goals are clear in your mind, it's easier to accomplish your "today" goals.

Concentration: how well you are focused on this moment and what's important now. Anything less than 100 percent concentration on what you are doing weakens your ability to succeed.

Confidence: your belief in your ability to reach your

goals. Confidence comes first from knowing you're doing what God wants you to do, but it also involves good preparation and presenting yourself well.

Challenge: the amount you demand of yourself. Your thoughts will rise to the level of your goals. Most people just want to push the easy button and get by on "okay." They think in terms of "good enough," and they avoid situations that require their best. Set high goals that demand a lot of you so that you will rise to meet them.

Not only will these four aspects of mental discipline help you succeed and experience great joy, but they will also make you a far more interesting and exciting person in the process.

LIVE 4:8 ::::::::::::::::::::::::::::::::

Work It

To help you focus on the joyous instead of the junky, write down on the following page three things you have done your very best on recently. In the box at the bottom, write, "I gave 100 percent, and it worked!"

Talk It

Tell someone that you don't want to push the easy button, but you want to give your best and reach for high goals. Ask him or her to text you "Don't push the easy button!" at a specific time later in the day.

1

2

3

Stick It: Thought of the Day

My thoughts
are clear and
focused.

 Pray It

Jesus, thank you for focused thoughts that help me meet my goals. Today, please remind me to give my best every moment so I can live the life you have for me. Amen.

EXTREME GRATITUDE

The Joy of Being Thankful

Stay alert, with your eyes wide open in gratitude.
COLOSSIANS 4:2, *THE MESSAGE*

MOST PEOPLE have a level of gratitude that is polite, nice, and
. . . normal. It includes saying thank you when someone gives
you a present, holds the door for you, or hands you your food
at the drive-through window. These are all situations where
most people express normal gratitude.

Some people have an immediate feeling of thankfulness
and relief when they hear about an accident. They feel bad for
the people involved, but grateful for their own safety and the
safety of their family and friends. This is also normal gratitude.
Wouldn't it be great, though, if we didn't need sad things like
accidents to remind us of our blessings?

The good news is, you don't! You can move to a whole new level of thankfulness that we'll call extreme gratitude.

Anyone can be thankful for something obvious, but it takes a joy-filled person to be grateful in a difficult situation. Being thankful for the smallest things that others don't see puts you in the extreme gratitude category.

When you're young, you tend to feel as if you will live forever. Life stretches out before you in years and years. It is easy to think that you can always do things right . . . tomorrow. You tell yourself there will be another day, but life doesn't always work out that way. Have you ever wondered if the victim of a car crash remembered to tell her family how much she loved them before she walked out the door that morning? Did she know how much they loved her?

Every morning, people all over the world walk out their front doors and never return home due to accidents, violence, weather, or other unpredictable situations. When you practice extreme gratitude, you have the peace of knowing that you have said what needs to be said and have expressed gratitude to the people in your life.

Extreme gratitude means being aware of blessings that we don't typically think about, things like the following:

- God's love
- your body
- your brain
- sunshine and rain
- forests and deserts
- mountains and beaches
- freedom in all forms
- technology

- relationships
- and much more

Extreme gratitude means being thankful for the "little" things in life, such as smiles, hugs, music, air-conditioning, heaters, clean water, science, education, seat belts, medicine, and second chances, to name just a few.

Extreme gratitude means telling people that you are thankful for them. Have you ever thanked your teachers for planning lessons and sharing their knowledge with you? Have you ever thanked your coaches for pushing you to excellence and getting you further than you ever would have gotten on your own? When was the last time you thanked your parents for loving you and taking care of you? Do you thank your close friends for their friendships or your Young Life leaders for spending time with you or your pastor for preparing and giving a sermon every week? These are the people who are investing in you. Honor them with your interest and attention. Think about their good qualities, and be thankful for those.

The more gratitude you give away, the more joy you get to keep.

LIVE 4:8 :::::::::::::::::::::::::::::::::

Work It

In the circles on the next page, write small things for which you are grateful. In the boxes, write the names of people for whom you are grateful. (You did something similar in Day 11. I would encourage you to choose four different people this time.)

Talk It

Thank God specifically for each of the small things you wrote down. Then come up with simple ways to thank the four people you listed for being important parts of your life. You can text, e-mail, Facebook, tweet, call, or whatever else you can think of.

Stick It: Thought of the Day

I express extreme gratitude.

Pray It

Heavenly Father, thank you for your awesome presence in my life and for all the blessings you have given me. Please help me to see all the goodness around me and to be extremely grateful. Amen.

CUT THE CLUTTER

The Joy of Simplicity

God is not a God of disorder but of peace.
1 CORINTHIANS 14:33, NIV

"THIS ROOM is a pigsty!" my dad said as he stood in the middle of my bedroom and looked around. I could have given excuses, such as the room was too small or I'd been too busy, but the truth was, I was disorganized. Piles of stuff were everywhere because I was too lazy to put it away or to throw it out.

It took me awhile to learn that clutter does not make me happy. It is distracting, tiresome, and frustrating. It gets in the way and makes simple tasks take longer. It smothers joy! Simplicity, on the other hand, grows joy. It makes life easier, more peaceful, and more carefree. Here is a simple formula to remember:

less clutter = more joy

Messy stuff can get in the way of what God wants you to do. Pieces of paper, gum wrappers, books, clothes, game discs, tennis shoes, headbands, and dirty socks piled all over keep you from thinking clearly and making good decisions. It is like gunk on your teeth that builds up over time. If you brush and floss daily, you can keep your teeth clean and healthy. If you don't, you get cavities. The same is true of your stuff. If you put it away daily and throw out or give away what you don't need, you can keep your life functioning well.

Clutter takes your attention away from what matters and gives it to what barely counts. When your room is full of things, you may find yourself thinking about those things all the time and seeking even more of it. Possessions become too important to you. Clutter turns your life and mind into a junkyard. Instead of focusing on what is lovely, pure, true, and worthy of praise, you are distracted by not being able to find what you need.

Picture the desk or table where you do most of your work. Then imagine you're on the yearbook committee, so you sit down and start working on some pages. You pull out your laptop to sort through photos. Then you print some pages you've designed and spread them out on the table to see how they look. After working on that for an hour, you push it to the side and take out the books you need to start writing a paper. When you're done with that, you shove the books over and get out the supplies you need for your art project. Pencils, paper, and erasers are scattered all over the work surface. By the time you start your fourth homework assignment, your desk is a mess and you can't find half of the things you need. You lose time searching for your assignment notebook or the right marker, and your frustration level rises. There is too much stuff trying to take up a small space.

That is how your life can be: junk all around you, stacked, pushed to the side, and scattered. It can be so overwhelming that you never want to clean it up. You end up doing less than your best in most areas, and you don't experience much joy. Clutter—whether physical or mental—limits our potential to be the people God created us to be because it robs our attention. The good news is that you don't have to live like that. You can take charge of your stuff and seek a simpler approach, releasing fresh creativity, joy, and energy.

Clutter piling up is going to happen from time to time, but how and when you deal with it is what matters. You have two choices: the chip-away method or the blitz method.

The chip-away method means you do a little decluttering every day. You spend ten to fifteen minutes daily putting things away or setting aside what you no longer need and can give away. The most practical times are probably when you get home from school and when you are getting ready for bed.

The blitz method is using larger chunks of time to clean up everything at once. Some people like to do this on Saturdays. They clean their rooms, bathrooms, and cars one time a week and it's done.

You know what works for you. The challenge is to do it consistently. Decluttering may not sound like fun, but the results are so worth it! Neat and clean are actually more fun. When your space is organized, your thoughts will be better organized too. And when your stuff isn't everywhere, you won't be constantly thinking about what you have and what new things you need. You'll start to enjoy simplicity, and you'll be able to think about more important things. That honors God and jump-starts your joy.

LIVE 4:8 :::::::::::::::::::::::::::::::::::::

Work It

Think about your bedroom, closet, bathroom, car, locker, and backpack. Do you have any clutter? On the next page, list the areas that need decluttering and imagine how having that space newly organized could help you. Think about your personality and the two choices: the chip-away method and the blitz method. Which will you use to declutter? In the box below the list, write the method you choose and when you will do it.

Talk It

Tell your parents about your plan to declutter. They will be more excited than anyone else in your life. If you share a room, your sibling might be pretty excited too.

Stick It: Thought of the Day

I keep it neat!

1

2

3

Pray It

Jesus, thank you for creating order and simplicity. Today, please show me how to live a more orderly life and to experience your joy and peace as a result. Amen.

PLUGGED IN

The Joy of His Presence

You make known to me the path of life;
*   you will fill me with joy in your presence,*
*   with eternal pleasures at your right hand.*

PSALM 16:11, NIV

GOD'S PRESENCE is everything good.

There is nothing more joyful than being with God. Talking to him and staying near him help us see our blessings. His presence is comforting, inspiring, encouraging, and strengthening, all at the same time. It helps us to see the difference between right and wrong, and it reminds us of how valuable we are and how much we are loved.

God's presence also shows us where to go and what to do, as well as where *not* to go and what *not* to do. From the goals you have been setting to the things you have been thinking to the choices you have been learning to make, it is God's presence that indicates when to say yes and when to say no. His presence in you helps you to see clearly both the truth and the lies in the world around you.

God is everywhere, but you have to reach out to him and think about him to experience his presence. When you don't feel close to God, it isn't God who moved or turned his thoughts from you—it's you. When your thoughts become stuck in sadness, anger, fear, or impurity, it's because you lost closeness with God, not because he lost closeness with you.

In this last day of our journey together, we are looking at the single most important habit you can put into your life to grow your joy: the daily choice to stay in God's presence. It works with everything else we have talked about. Nothing does for us what being near him does, but it takes practice. Like any close relationship, your connection with God needs attention to stay healthy.

God is always with you, as he says in Hebrews 13:5: "I will never leave you; I will never abandon you" (GNT). But you don't always feel his nearness. When your mind becomes busy with daily details, you can lose your awareness of him. You have a lot of conversations with your friends that aren't about God, and you read books for school that aren't about him. Unless you make an effort to think about him, you probably won't. And when you aren't thinking about him, you miss the good things he has for you. You don't want that!

Learn to practice the presence of God no matter where you are or what you are doing. There are three simple steps that will help, if you will make them part of your daily life:

Think about God. Remind yourself often of what is true about him. For example, God is love. God is all-powerful. God is always with me. God knows everything. God knows me. God is truth. God is holy. God is faithful. God is patient. God is my joy. God does what is right. God never changes. God forgives me. God is for me.

Praise him like that in your thoughts. Let the things you know about God move through your mind all day.

Talk to God. He is right there with you, waiting for you to say something. Start conversations with him anytime during the day. Tell him how you are feeling or what you need help with. Use normal words, just as if you were talking to a friend. When you talk with God throughout your day, it helps you feel connected to him, it helps you hear him, and it helps you feel alive in every moment.

Read about God. The most awesome thing about you is that God is in you and working in you. That happens as you consistently read his Word. God's words shape your thoughts and attitudes, making every day more joyful and more filled with purpose. A fun way to make the Bible come alive is to put your name in the verses. Make them your own! After all, God is talking to *you*. Consider these promises:

- Christ has come so that I, [insert your name], might have life, and have it more abundantly. (See John 10:10, NKJV.)
- God has not given me, [insert your name], a spirit of fear, but of power and of love and of a sound mind. (See 2 Timothy 1:7, NKJV.)
- God takes great delight in me, [insert your name]; he will quiet me, [insert your name], with his love; he will rejoice over me, [insert your name], with singing. (See Zephaniah 3:17, NIV.)

God's presence satisfies you. Without it, nothing will satisfy you. Nothing and no one can take his place. The more you practice his presence, the more you will experience your life and the world through Philippians 4:8.

And joy is the result.

Fix your thoughts on what is true and good and right. Think about things that are pure and lovely, and dwell on the fine, good things in others. Think about all you can praise God for and be glad about.

PHILIPPIANS 4:8 (TLB)

LIVE 4:8 :

Work It

In your own words, describe three simple ways you will stay close to God.

1
2
3

 Talk It

Out loud by yourself, practice putting your name into some verses. You can use the ones given as examples or start with Psalm 139:13-18.

Tell someone what this forty-day journey has done in your life . . . then go spread the joy!

Stick It: Thought of the Day

God is here, right now, waiting for me!

 Pray It

Heavenly Father, thank you for always being with me. Please help me to practice your presence and stay close to you all the time. Amen.

About the Authors

TOMMY NEWBERRY is the founder and head coach of The 1% Club, a life-coaching firm that helps entrepreneurs maximize their full potential in all areas of life. Since 1991 Tommy has equipped business leaders in more than thirty industries leverage their strengths, maximize their influence, and enjoy greater satisfaction with the right accomplishments. Beyond just business, his annual Couples Planning Retreat and Big Picture Parenting programs help husbands, wives, and parents stay focused on what matters most.

He is the author of several books, including the *New York Times* bestseller *The 4:8 Principle* and the motivational classic *Success Is Not an Accident*, both of which have been translated into multiple languages. Tommy has appeared on more than two hundred radio and television shows and is frequently invited to speak at business conferences, schools, and parenting groups. He lives in Atlanta, Georgia, with his wife, Kristin, and their three boys. Connect at www.tommynewberry.com.

LYN SMITH is a truth teller who brings the reality and power of God into daily living. After twenty years of leading and teaching in Bible Study Fellowship International, she began speaking and writing on her own in 2010. Traveling the world, she teaches at pastors' conferences, women's conferences, churches, and rehabilitation centers. She appears weekly on Christian Discipleship TV. A contributor to *The LeadHer Challenge,* she is currently writing her third book. Lyn lives in Oklahoma City with her husband and three children. Connect at www.lynsmith.org.

DISCOVER THE SECRET TO A JOY-FILLED LIFE!

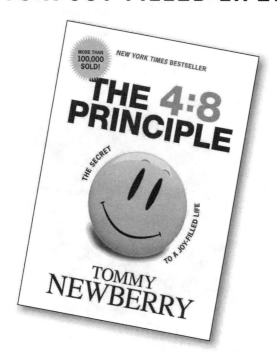

Want to live a happier, healthier, more successful life?

Here's the good news: It's all within your grasp—
and it's easier than you think.

Unlock the power of *The 4:8 Principle* today.
It will forever change the way you think and live!

Now available in stores and online.

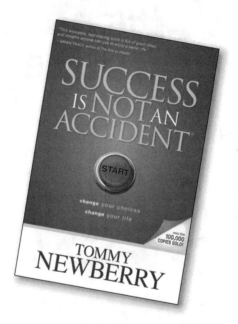